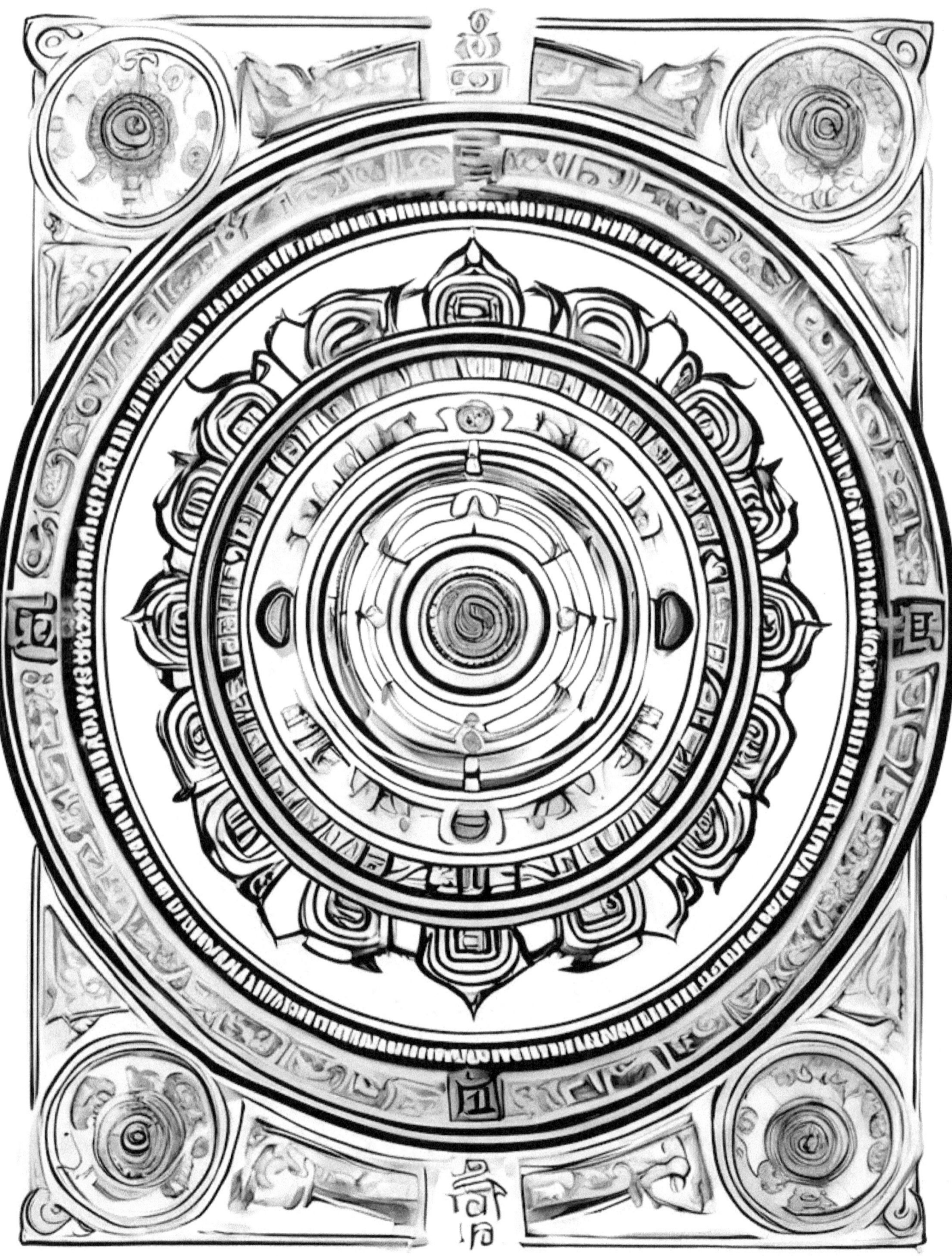

In the silence of the Tibetan valleys, where the winds carry the echoes of ancient spiritual traditions, mandalas emerge as visual expressions of the harmony between the mind and the universe.

Every line, every curve, is an invitation to an inner journey, a portal to contemplation and peace.

When you start coloring, remember that each stroke is a step towards inner peace.

Let yourself be enveloped by the peaceful energy of the mandalas and allow the colors to intertwine, forming a silent dialogue between your soul and the art.

Just as a Tibetan monk takes time to create a sand mandala, dedicate precious moments to coloring and finding balance within yourself.

Namaste.

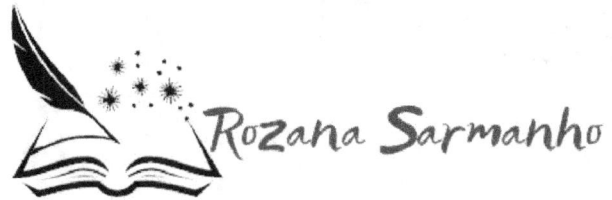

Rozana Sarmanho

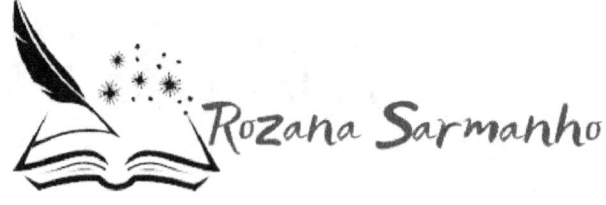

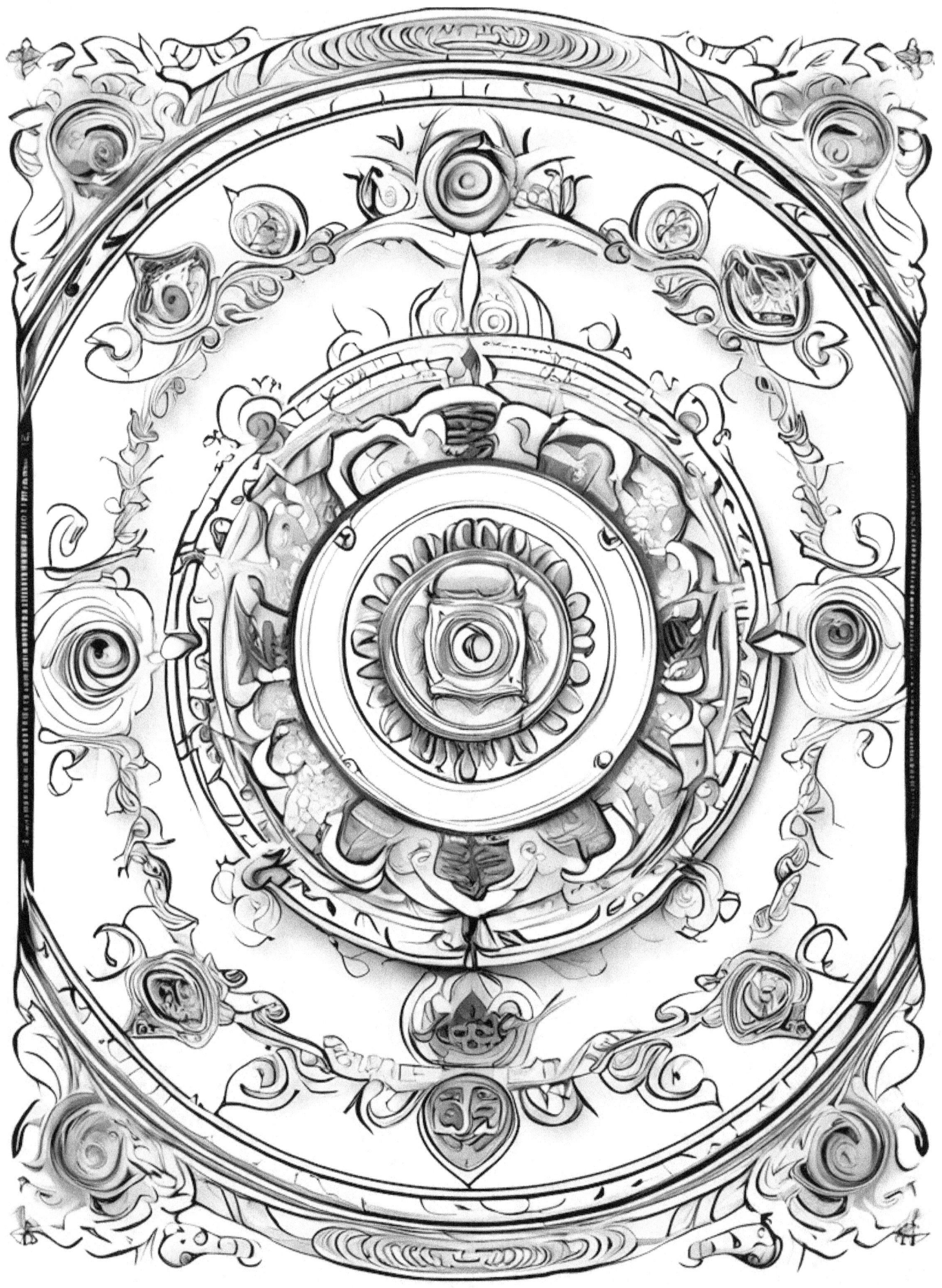

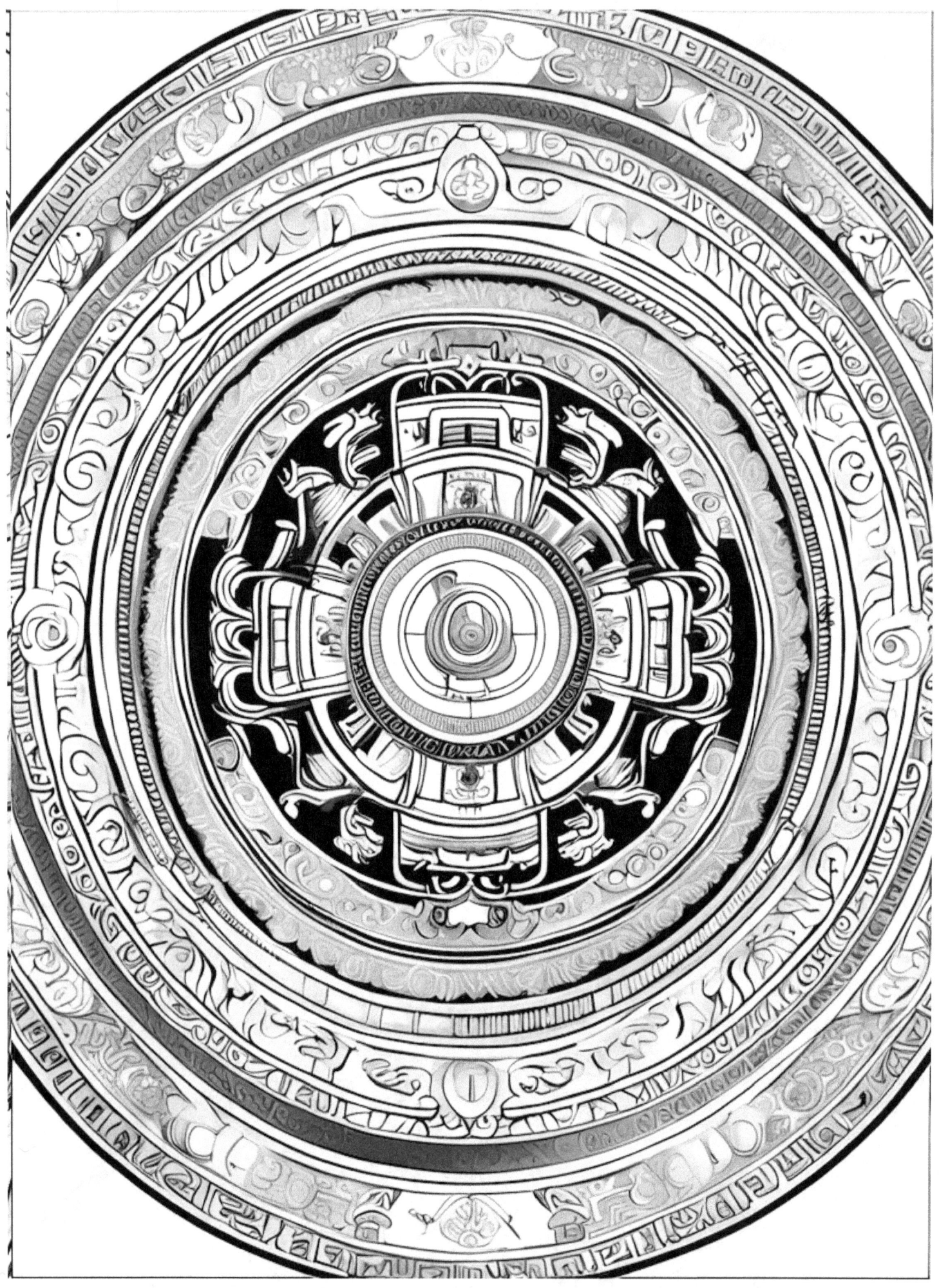

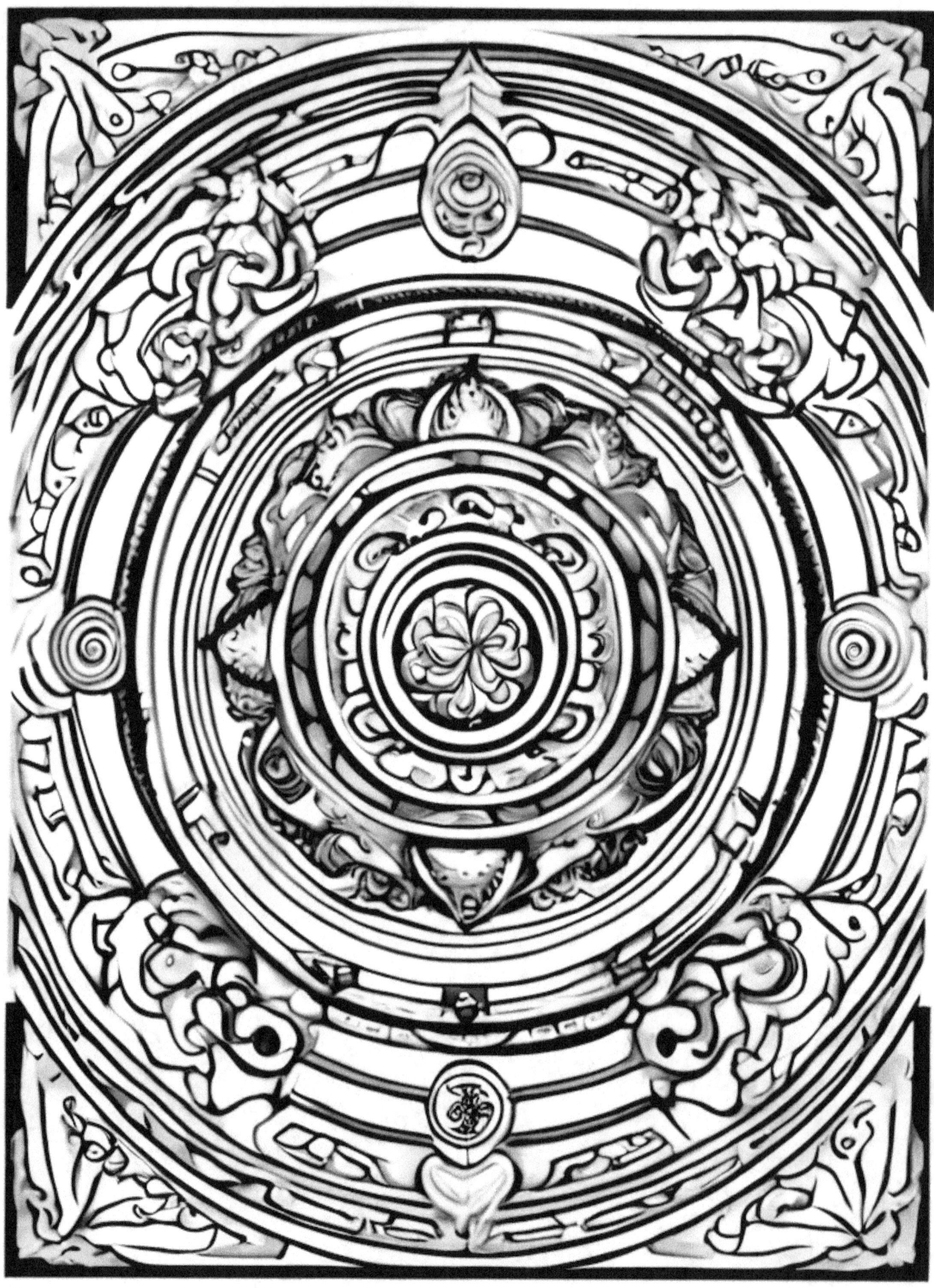

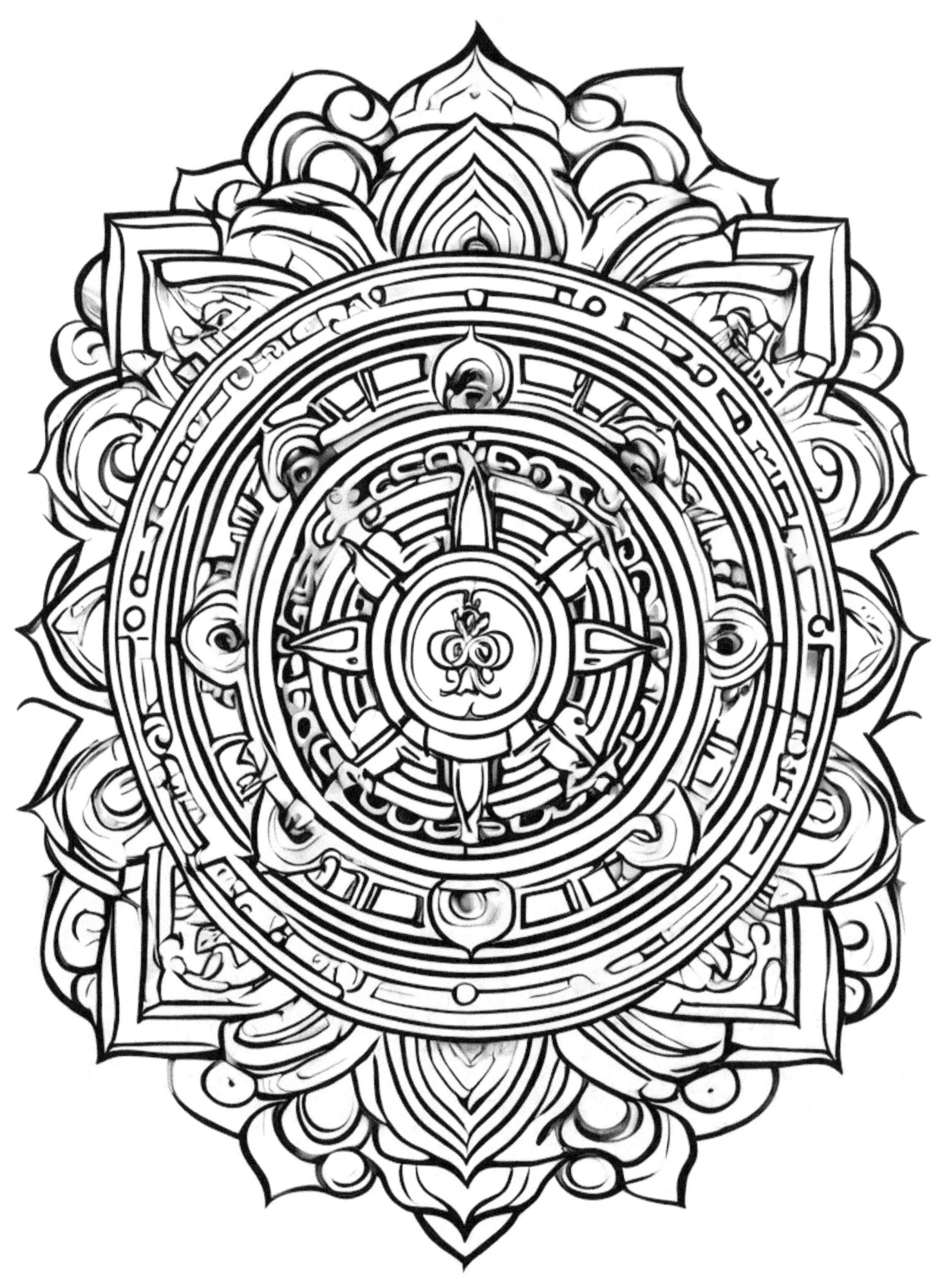

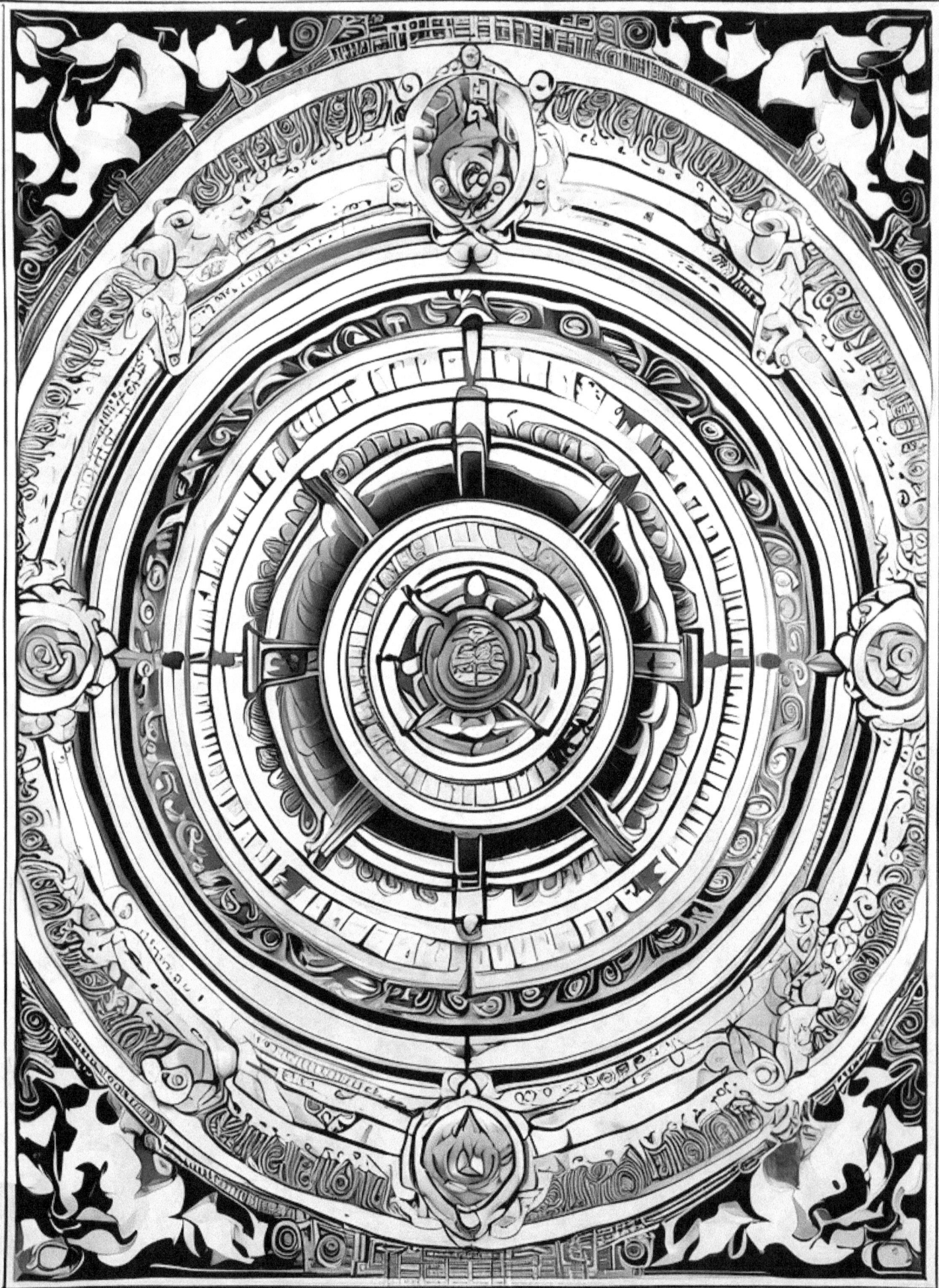

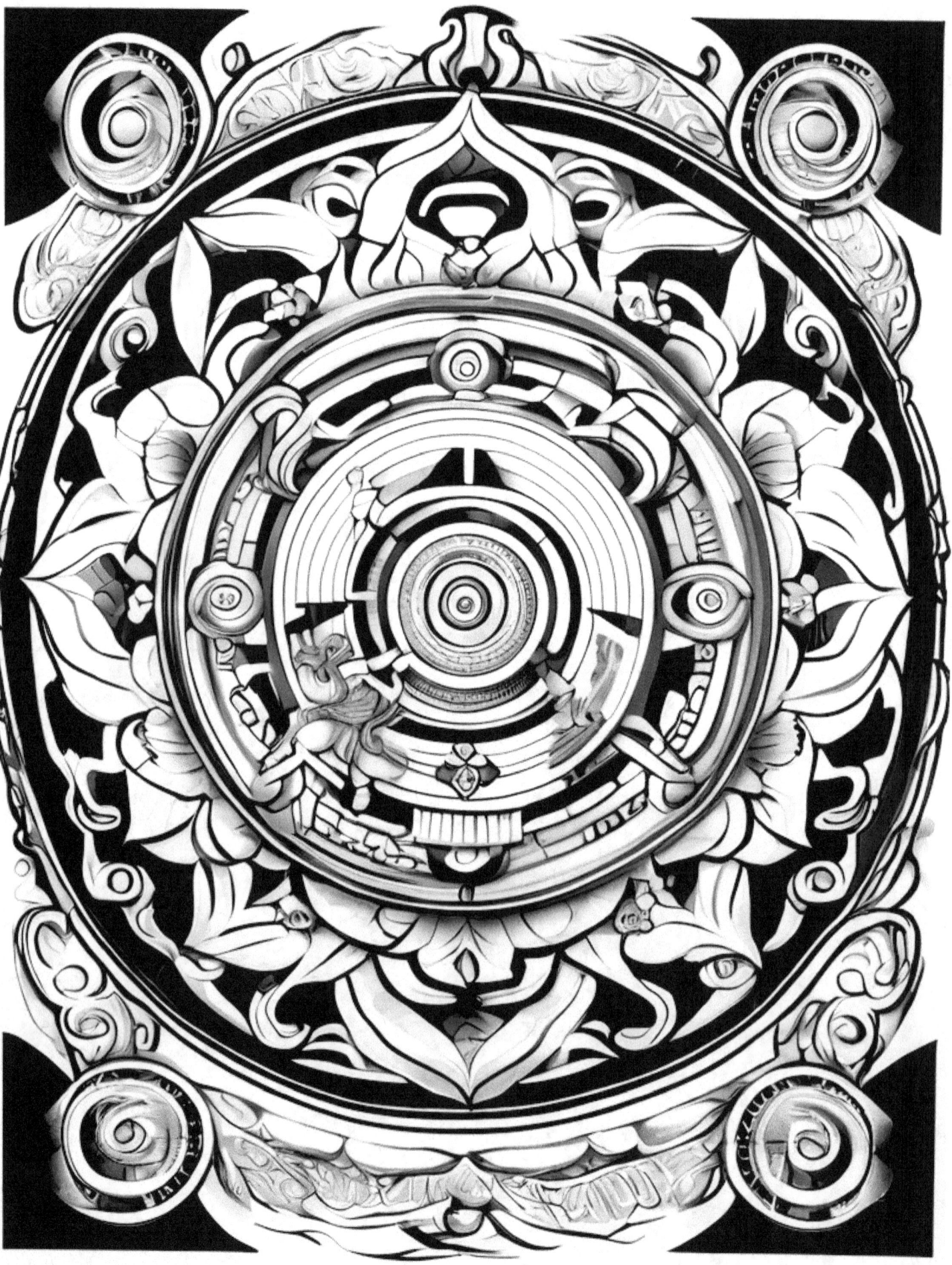

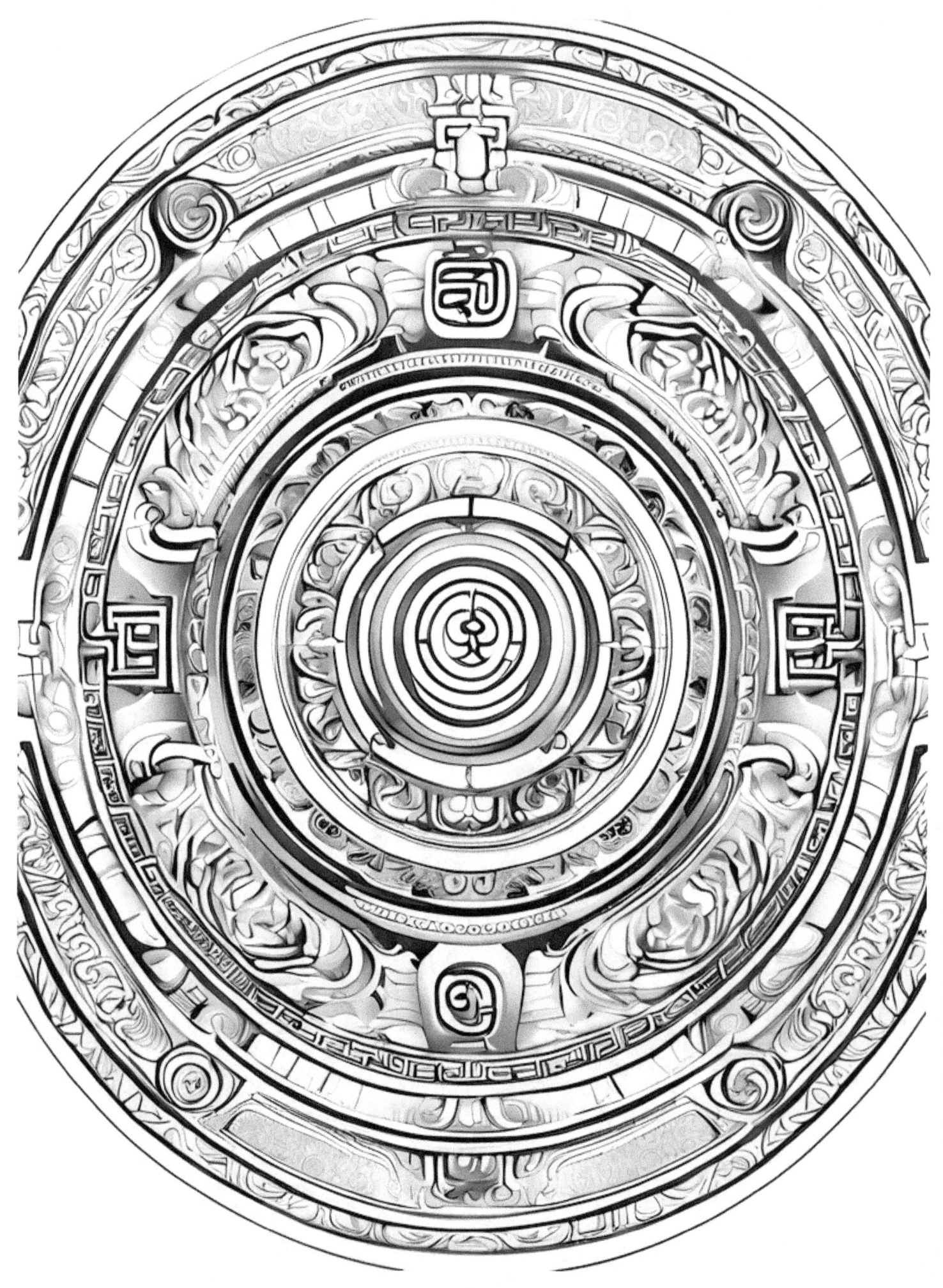

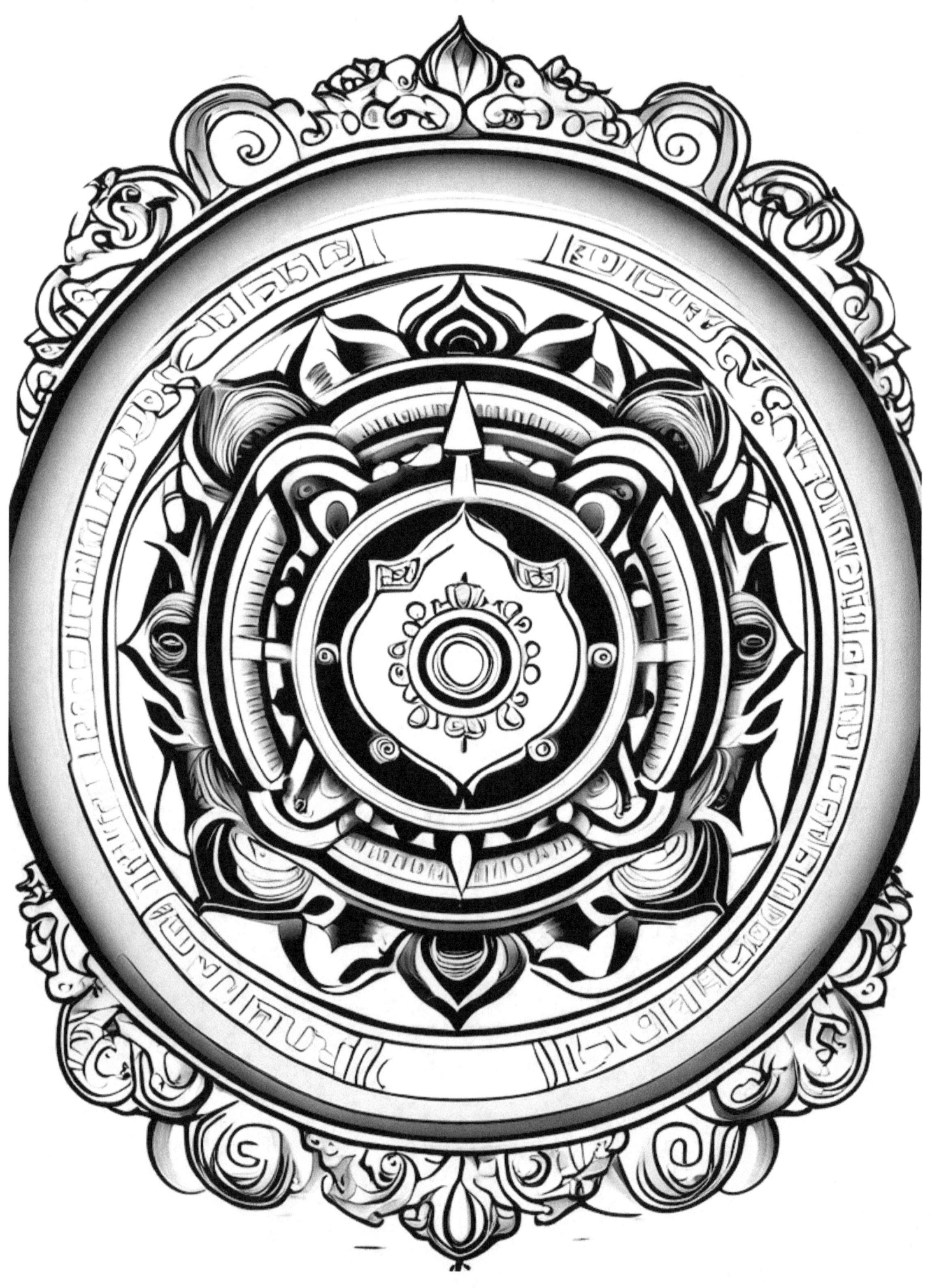

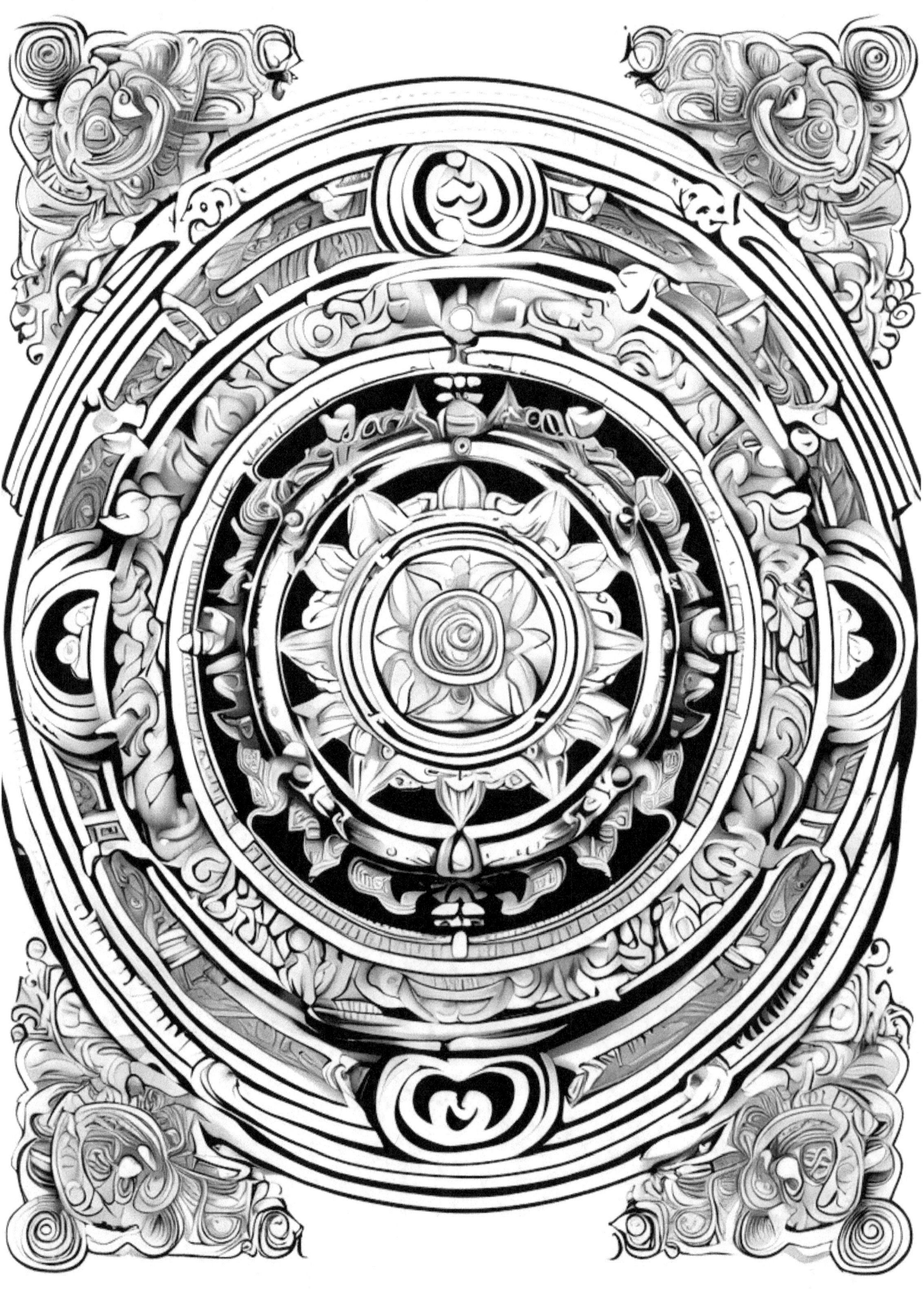

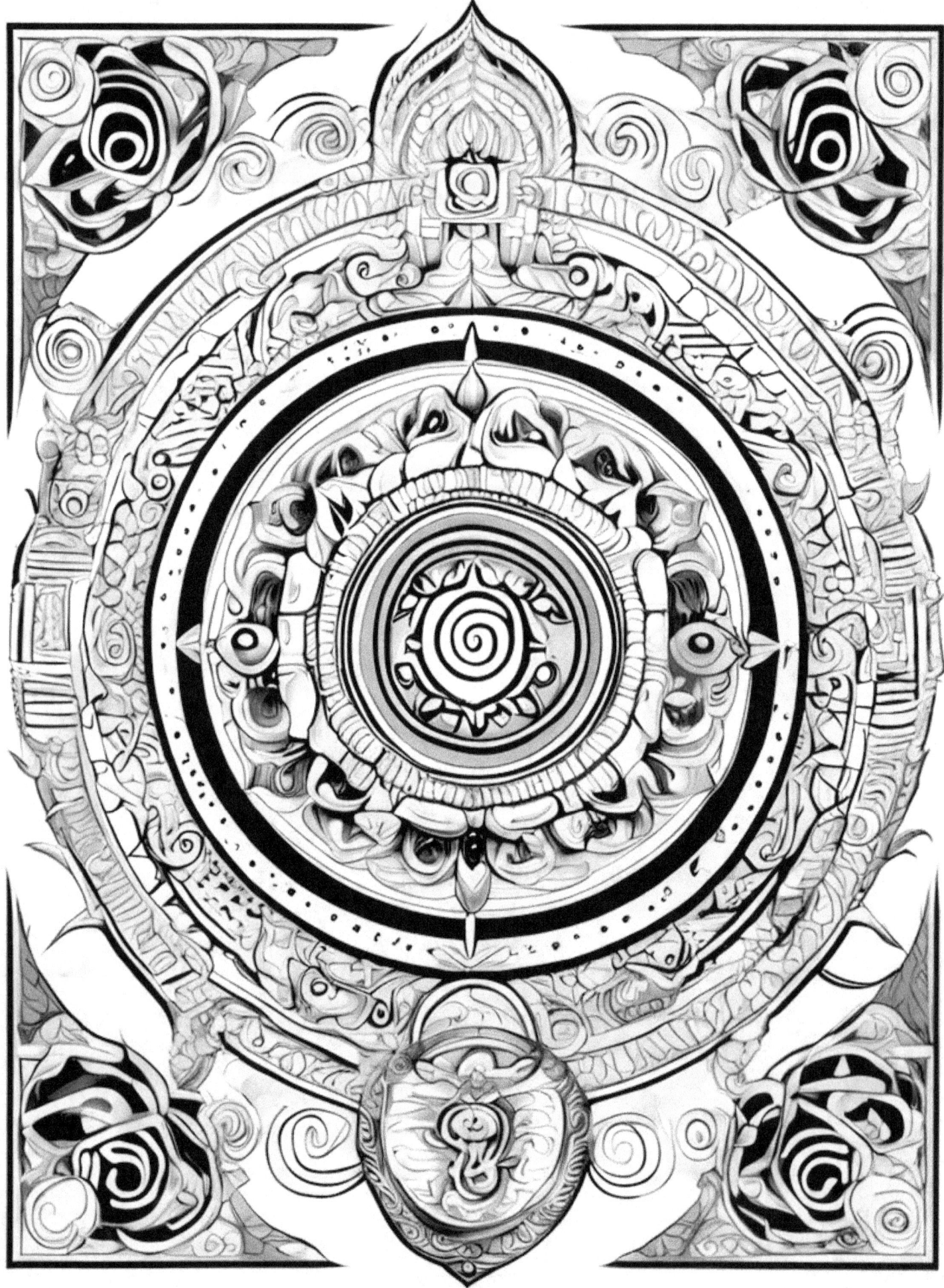

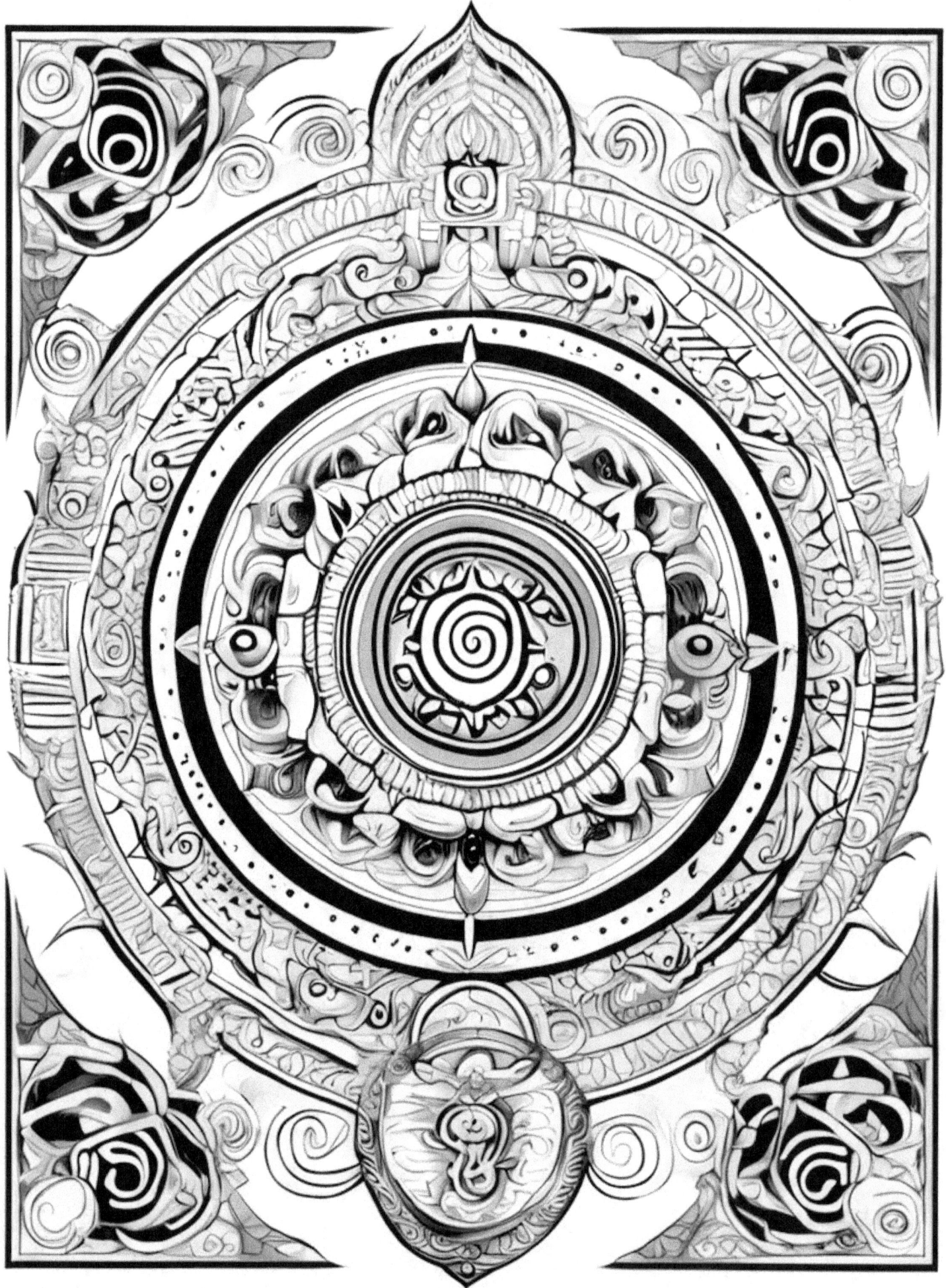

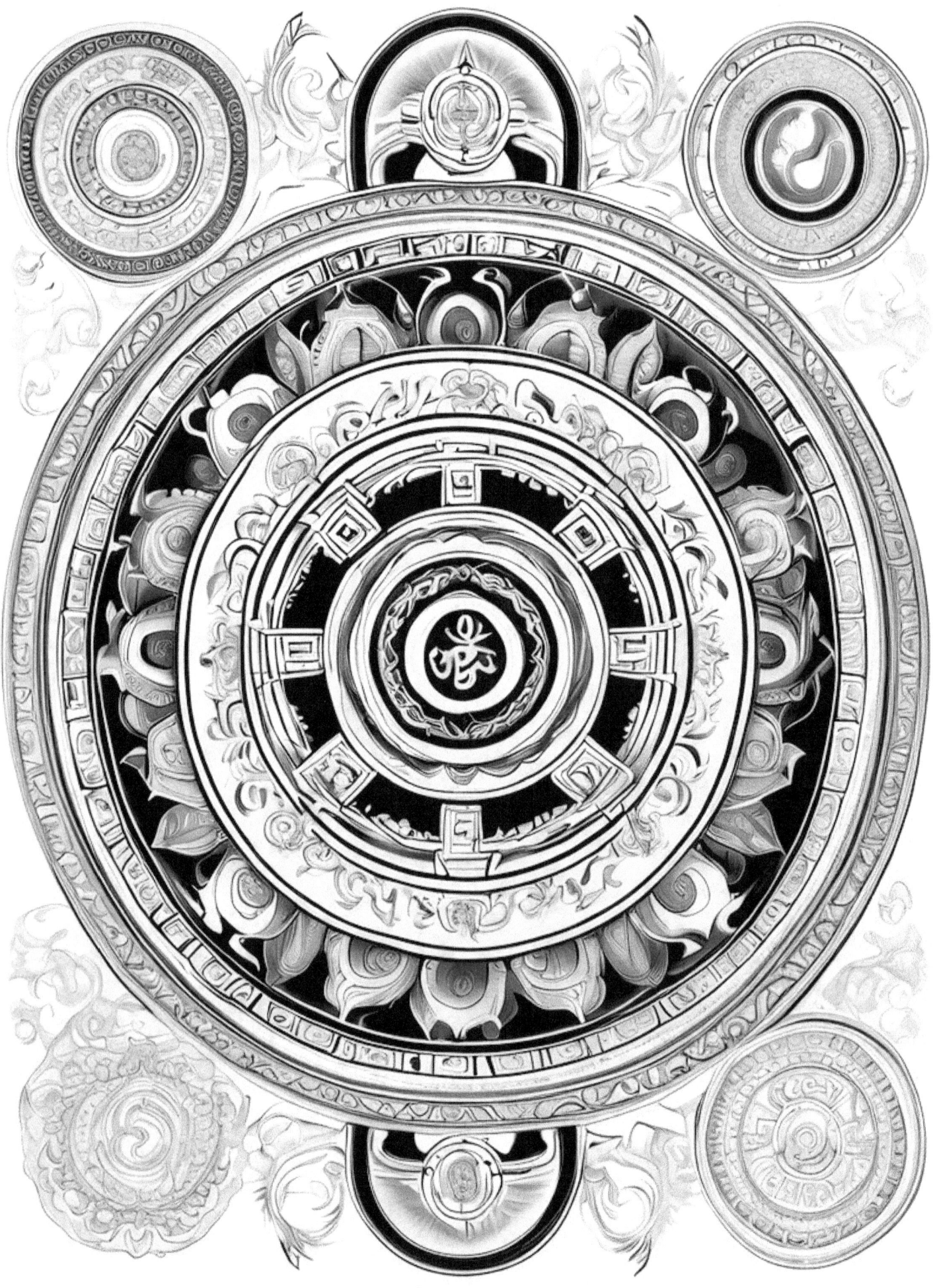

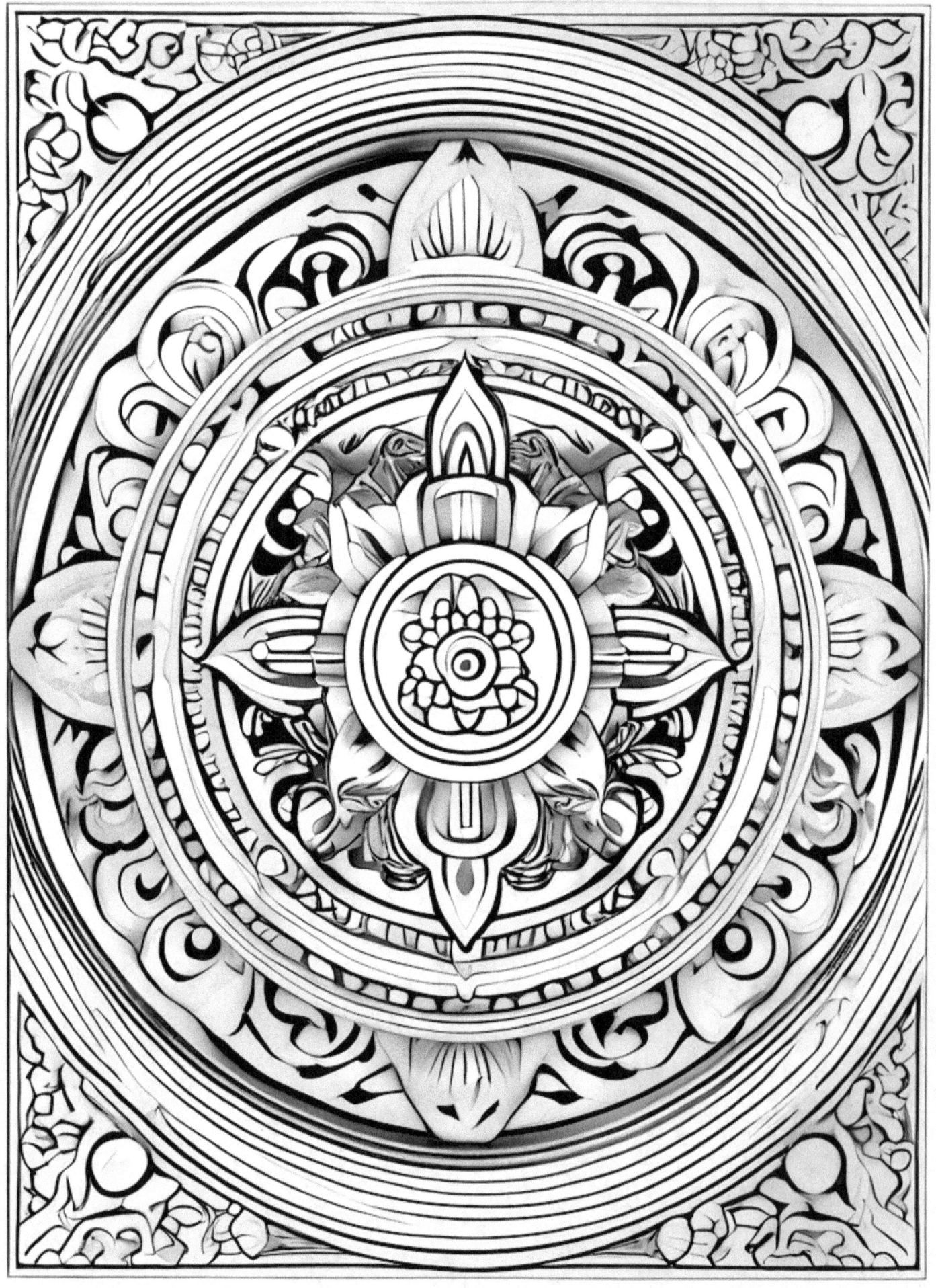

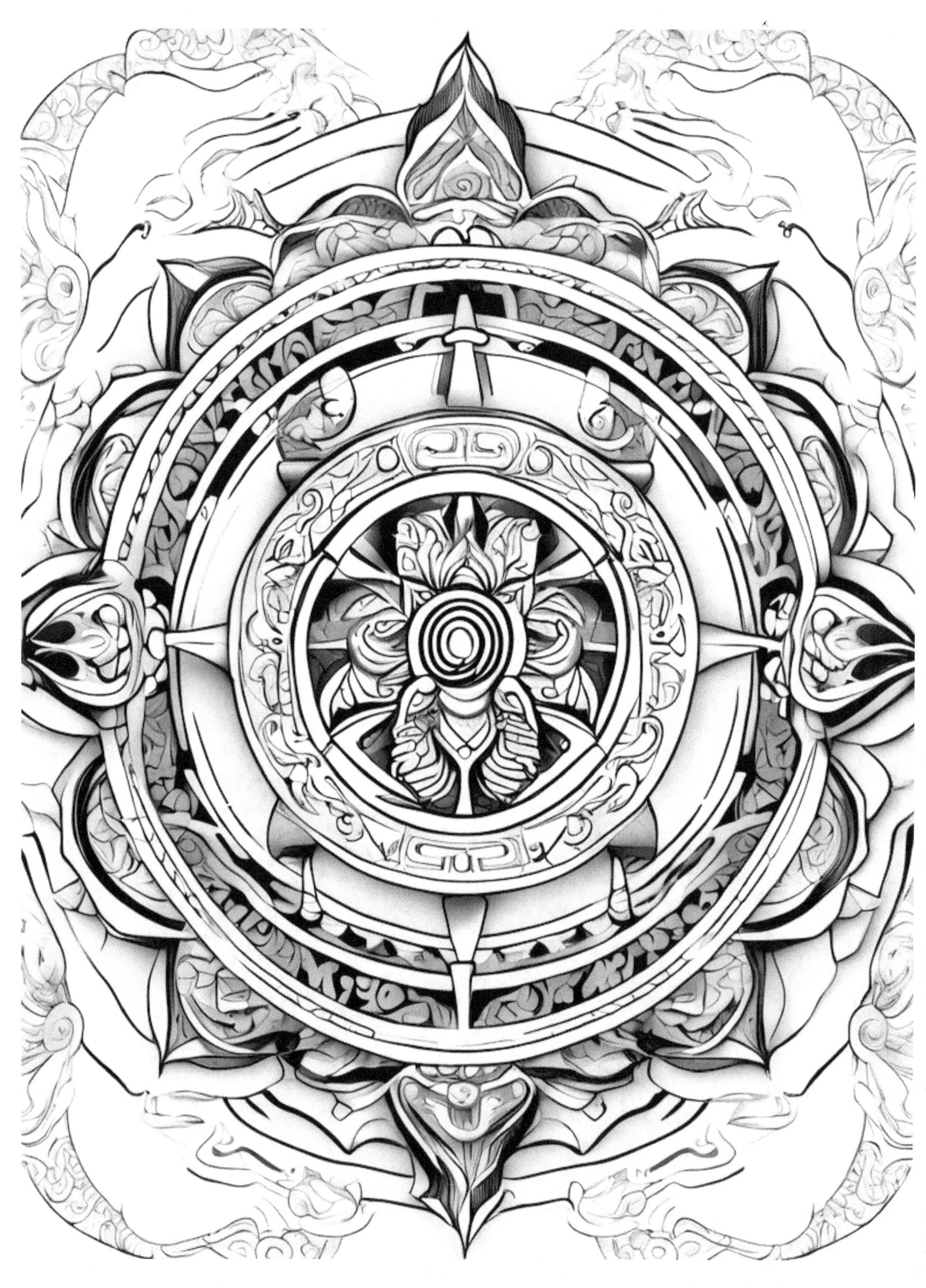

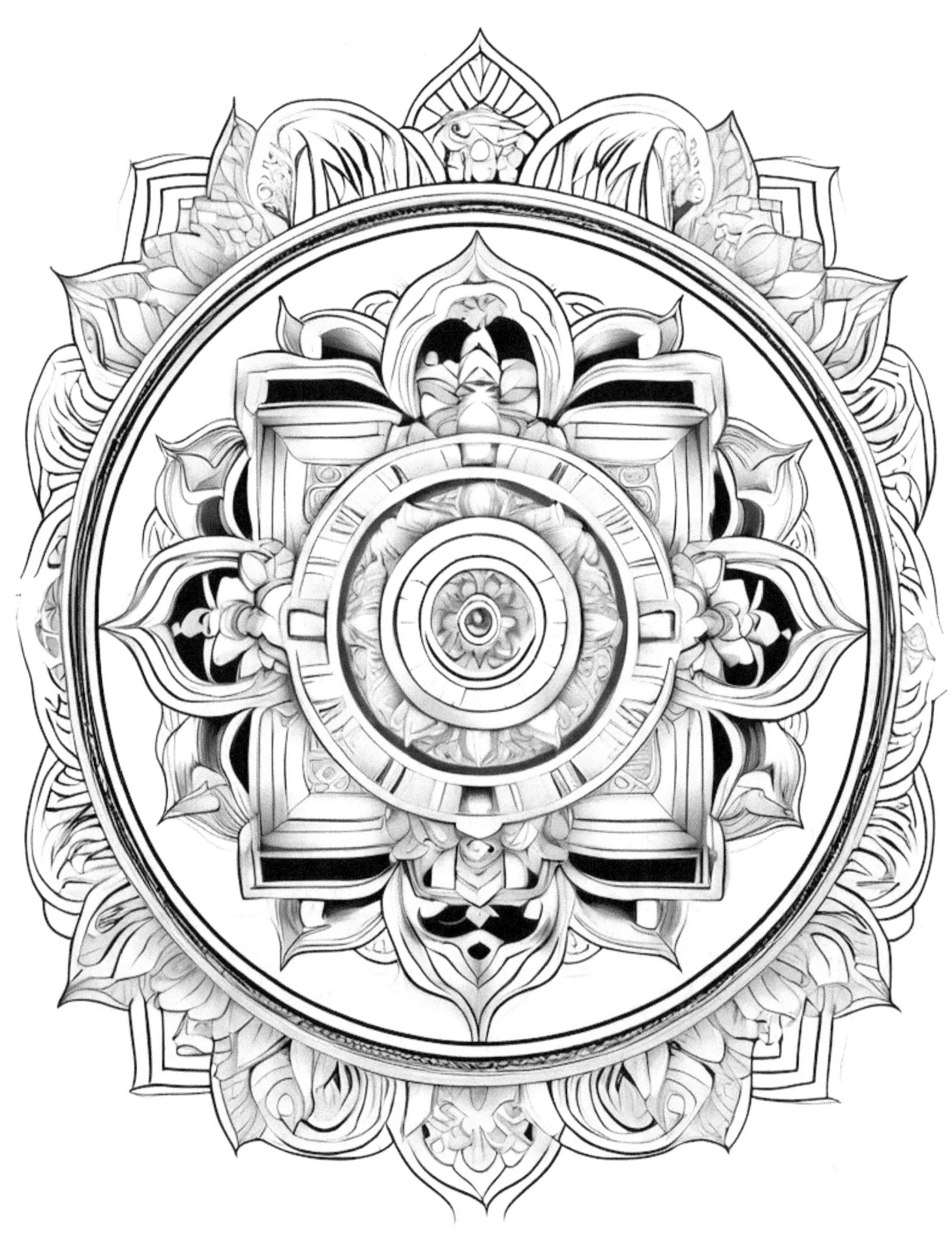

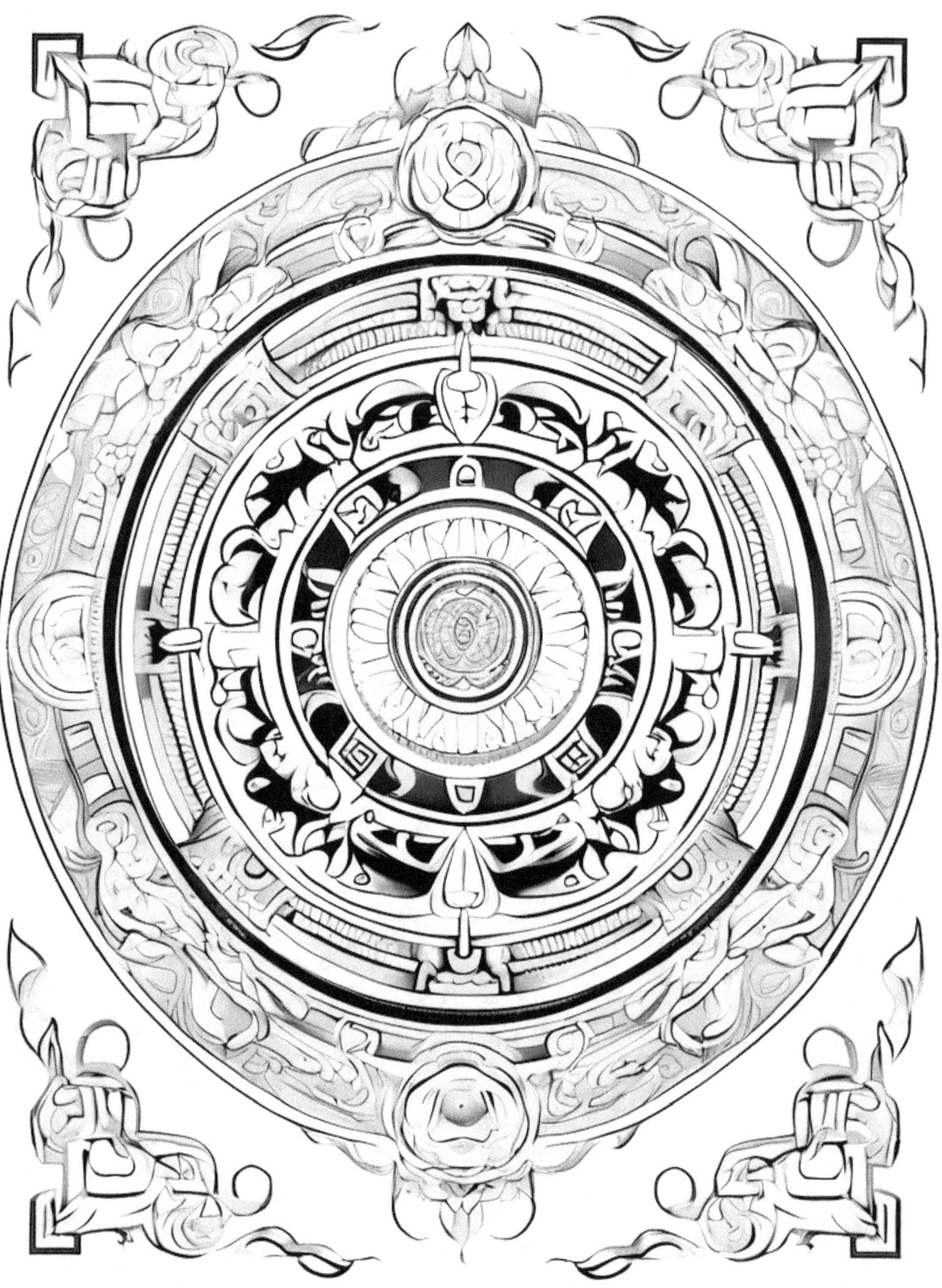

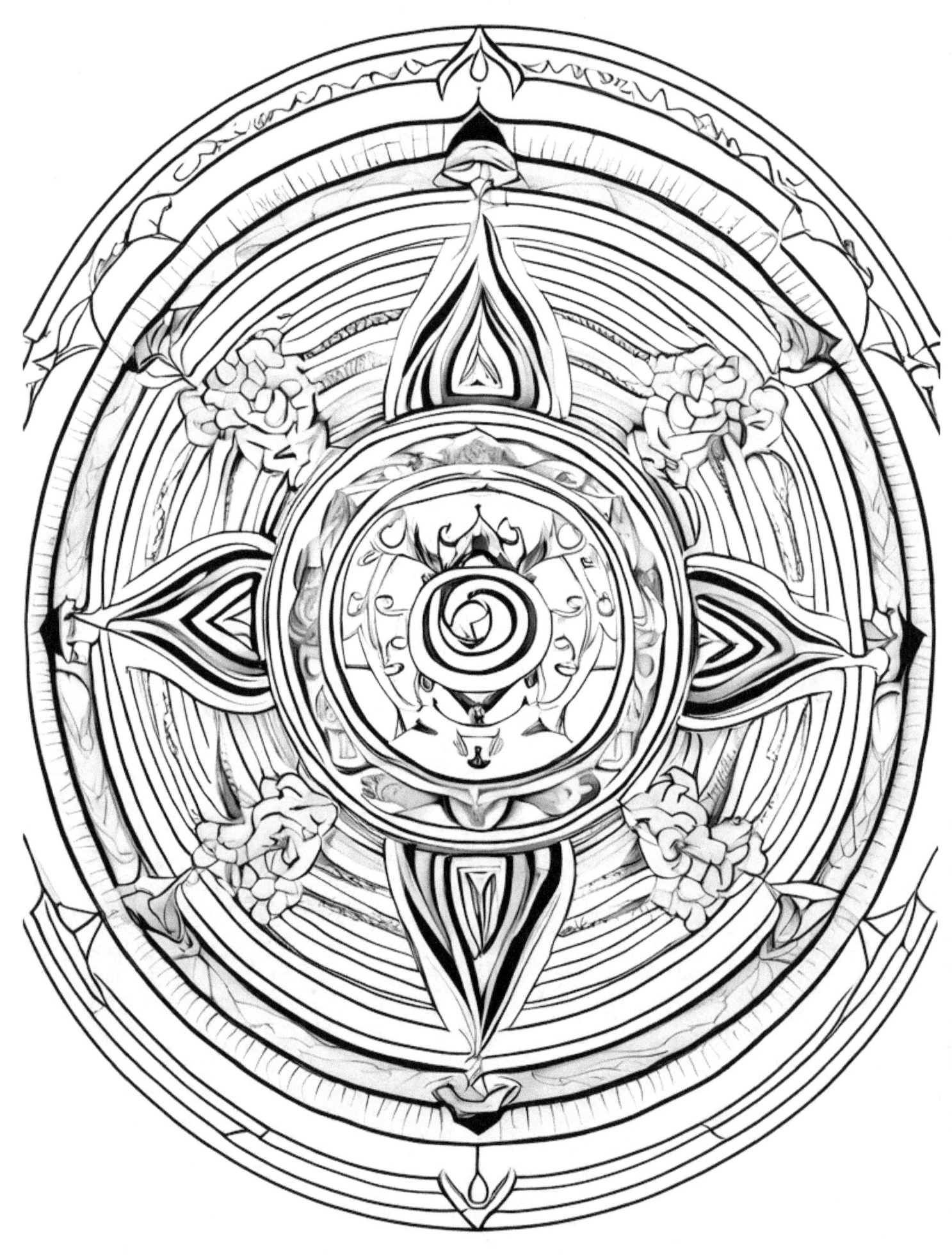

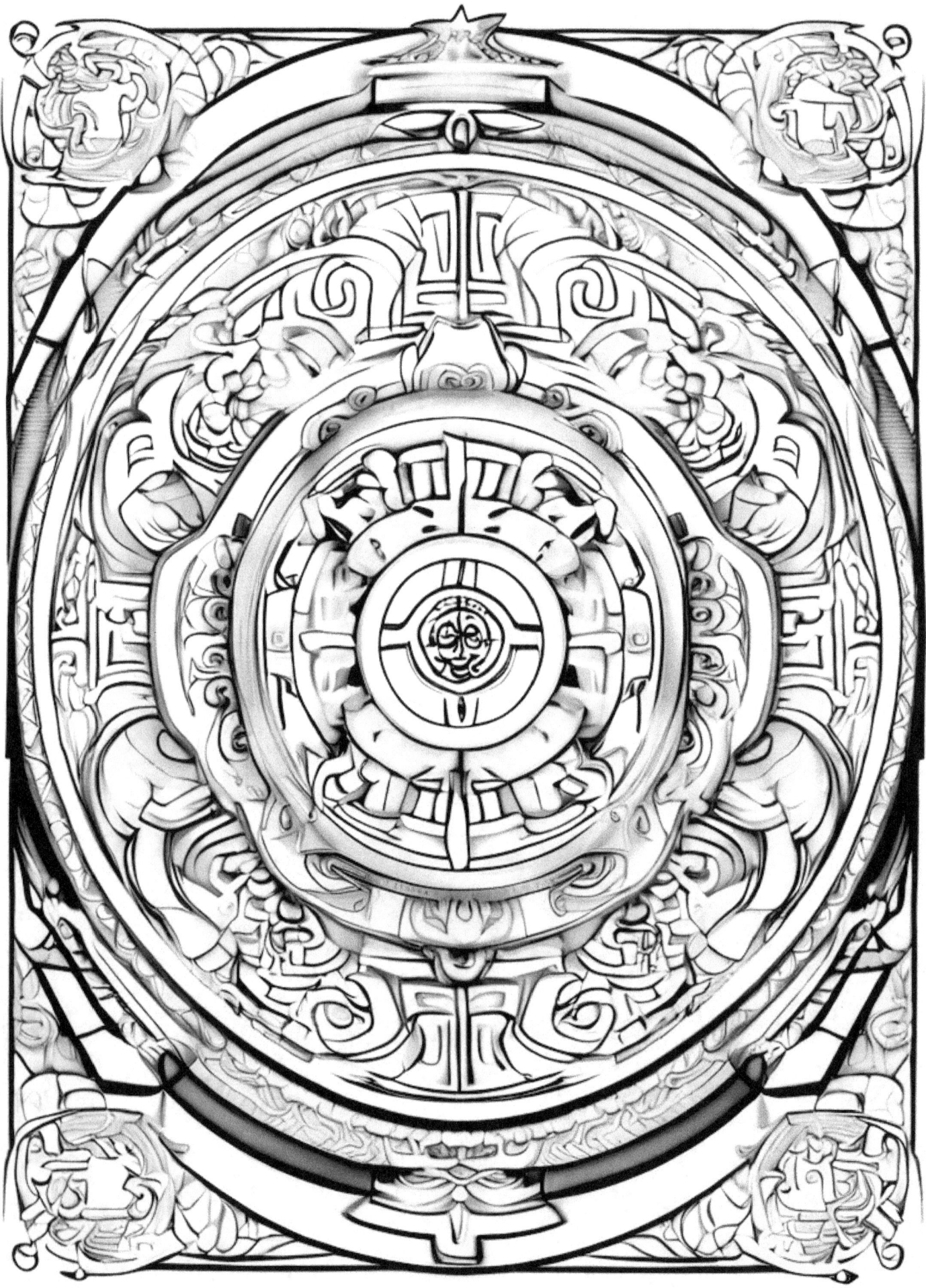

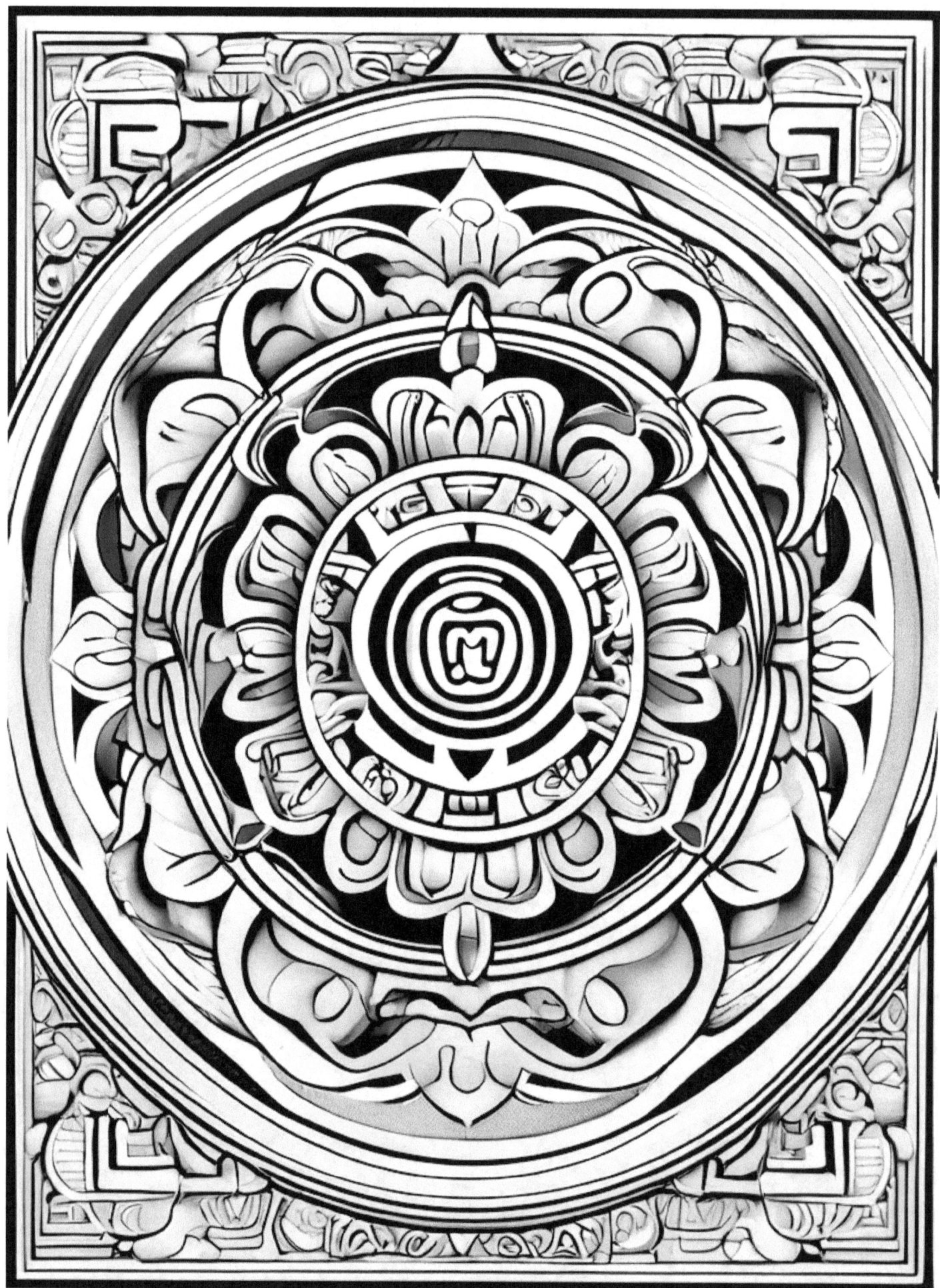

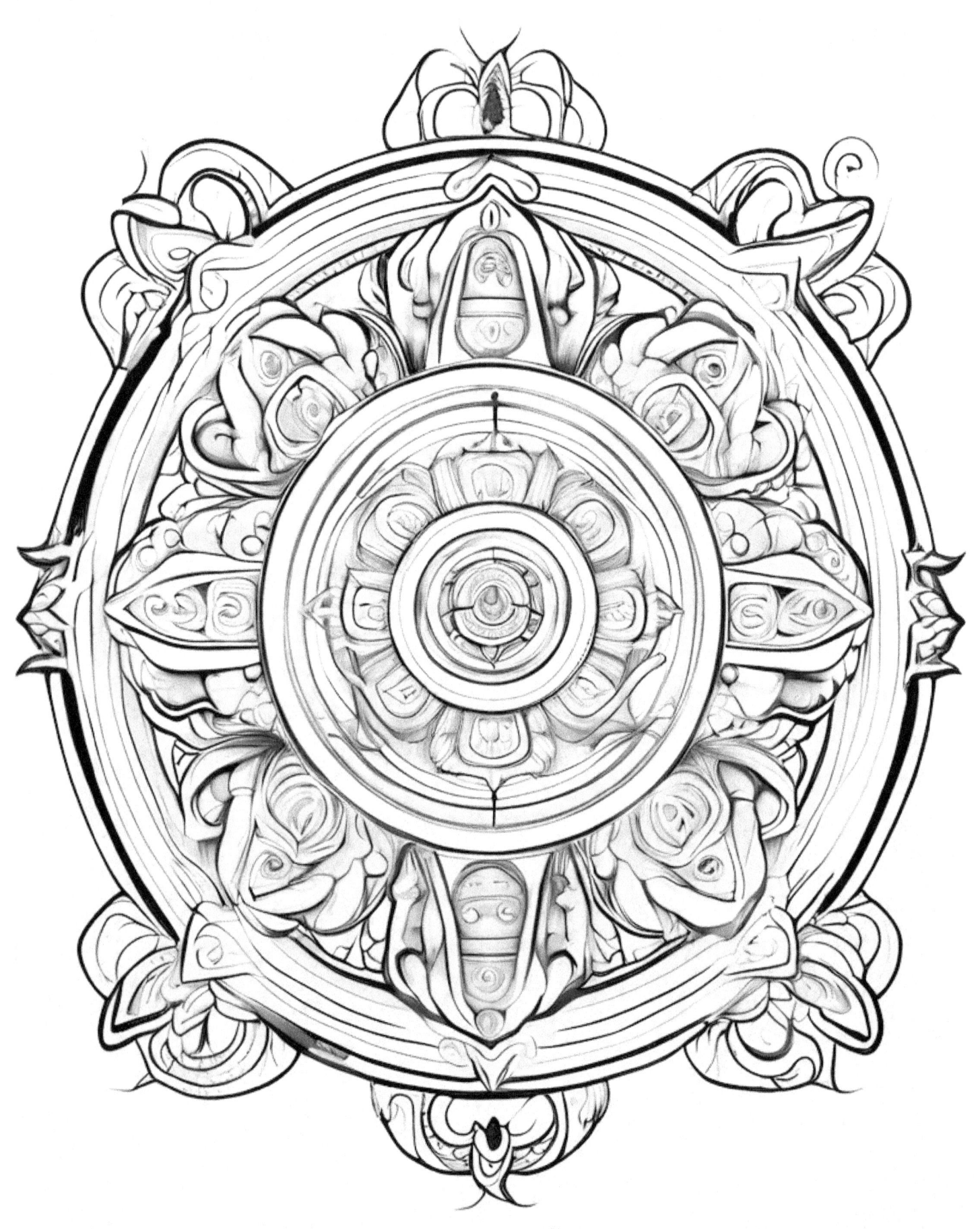

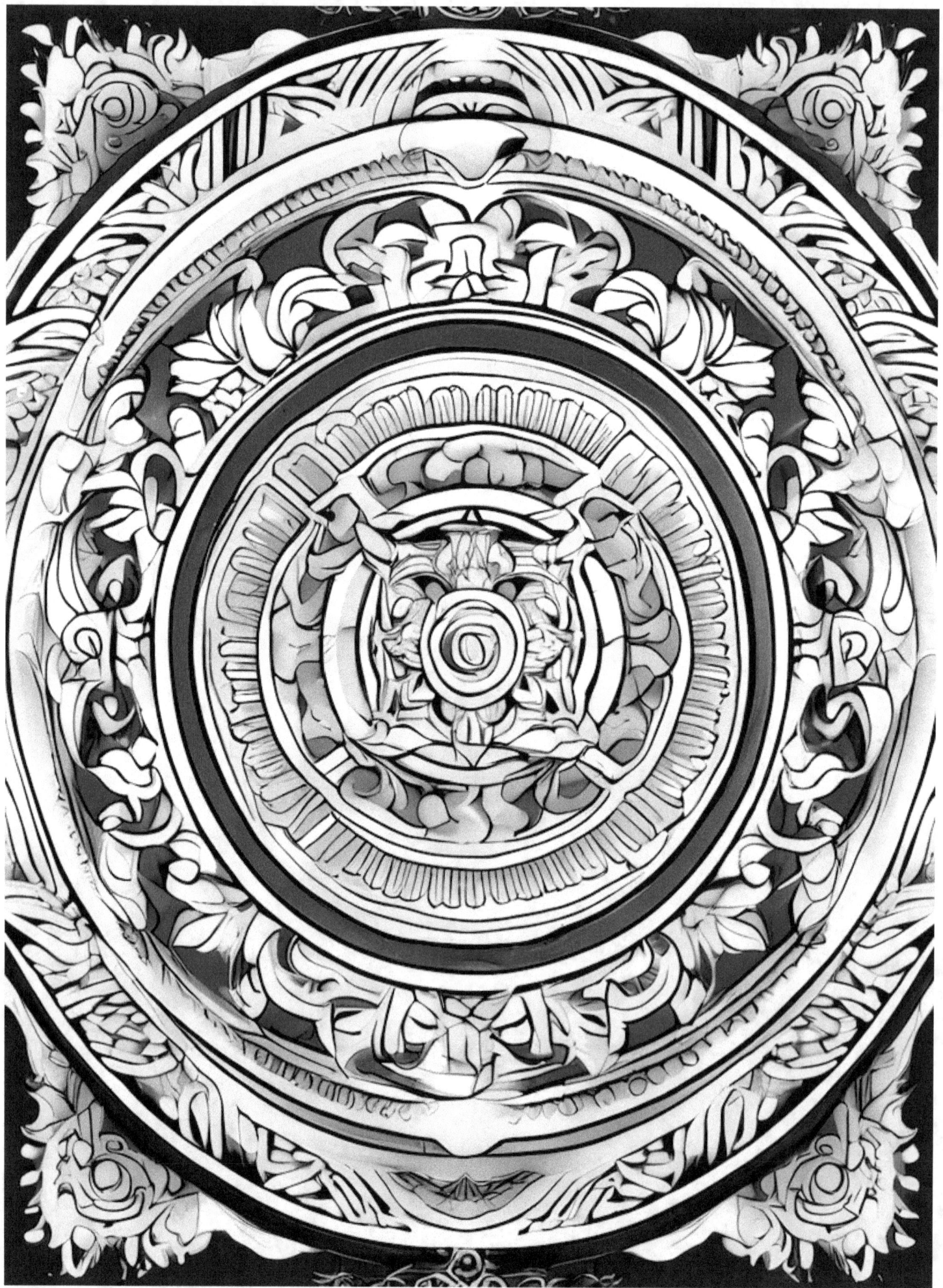

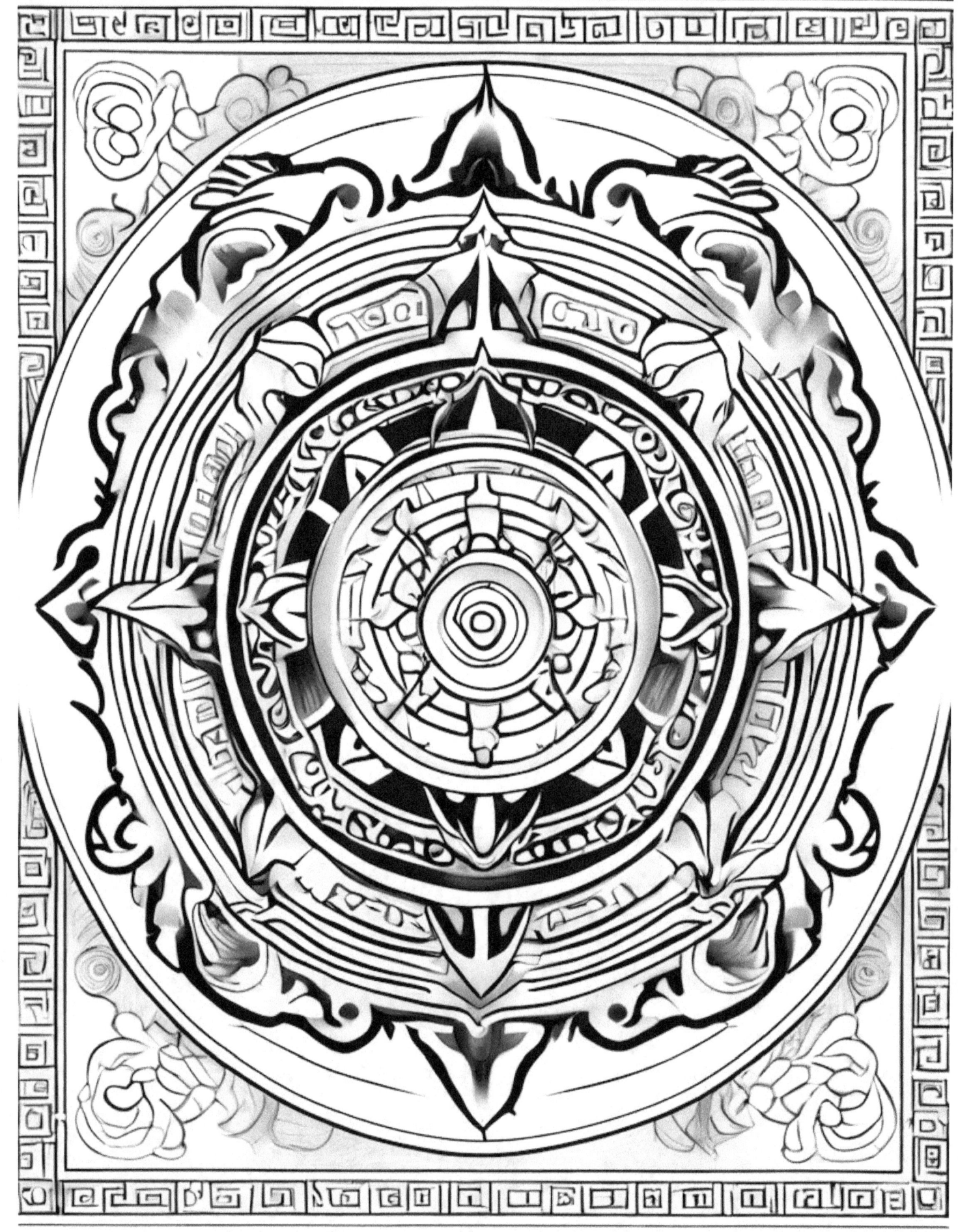

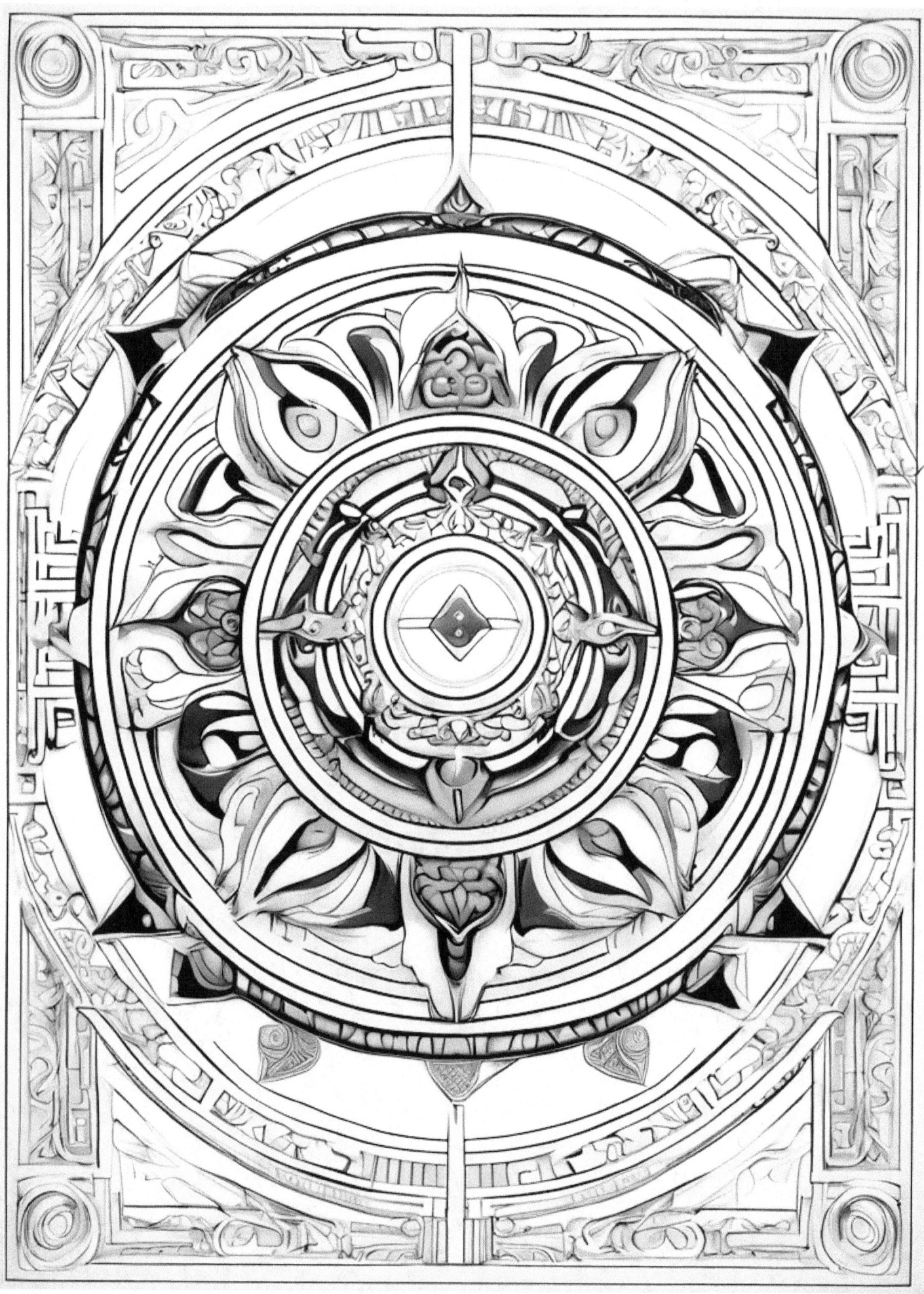

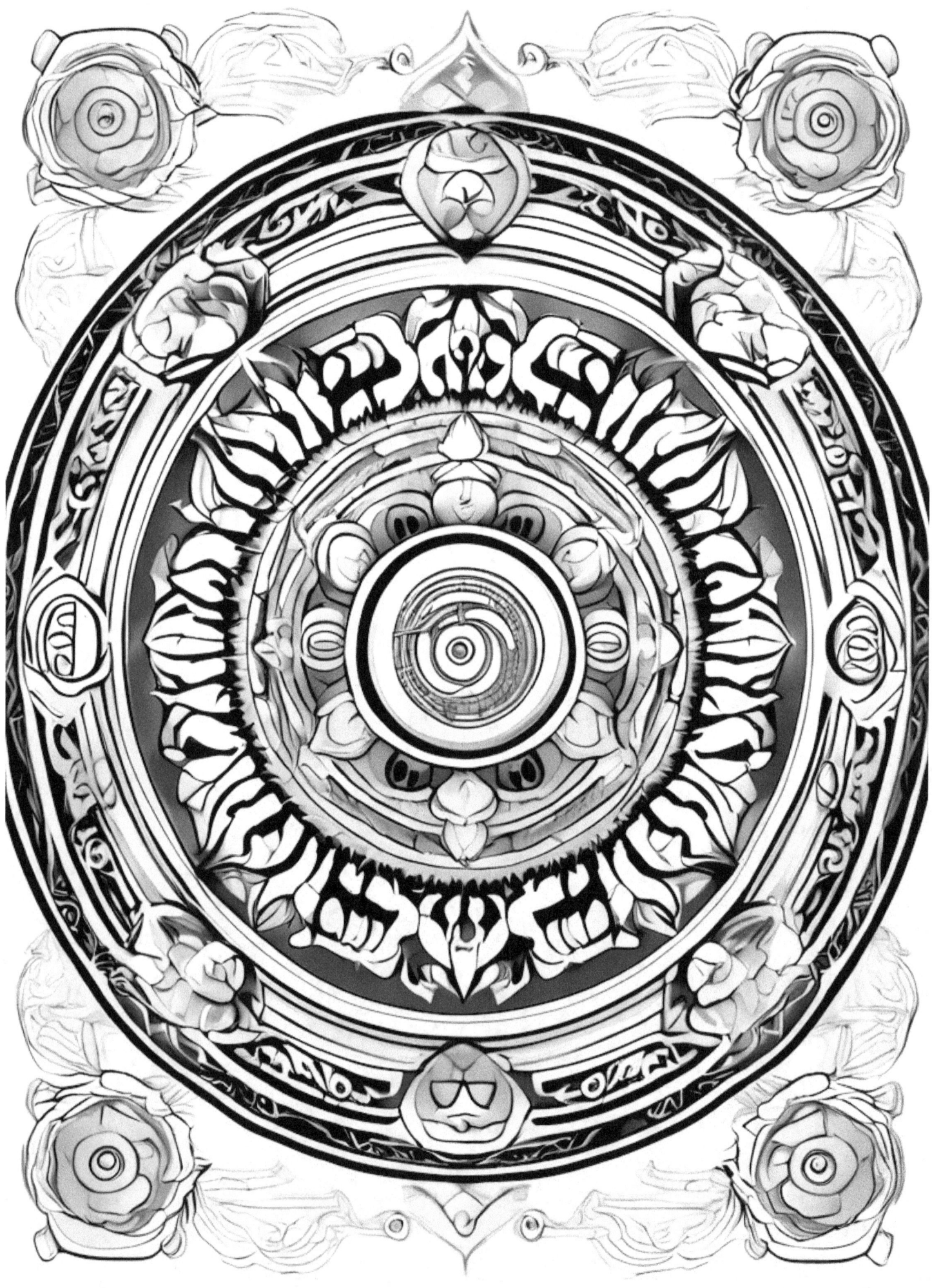

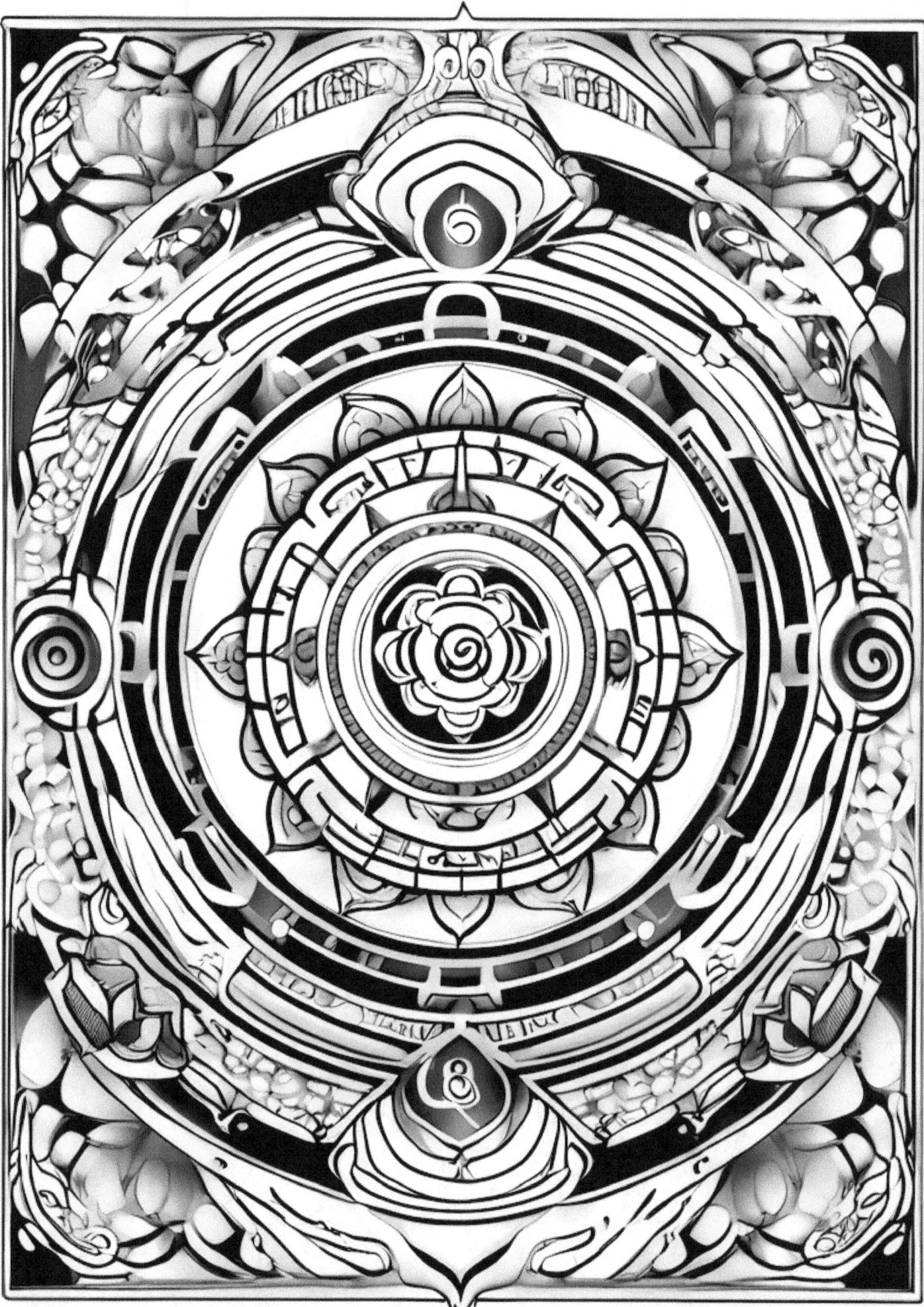

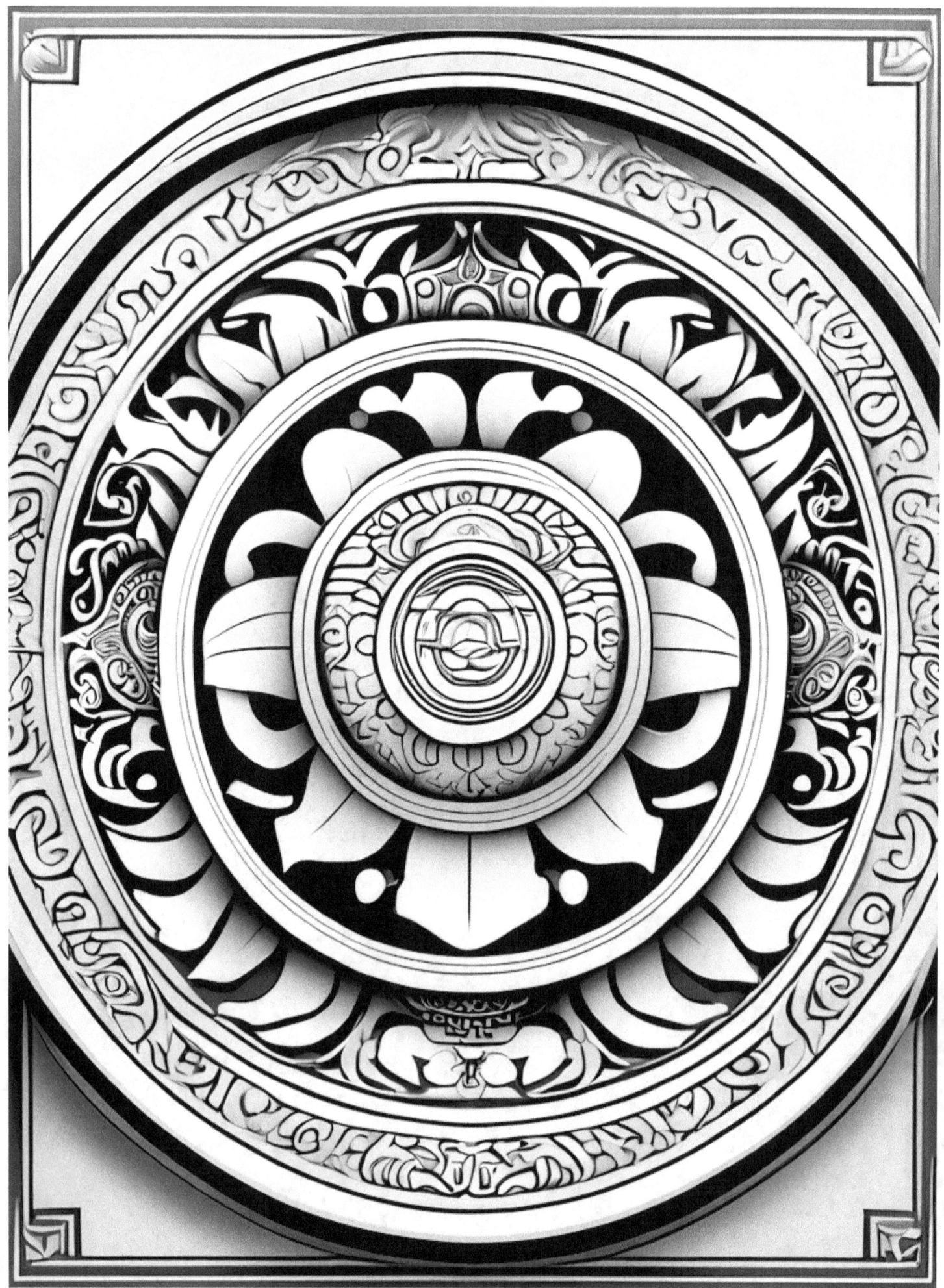

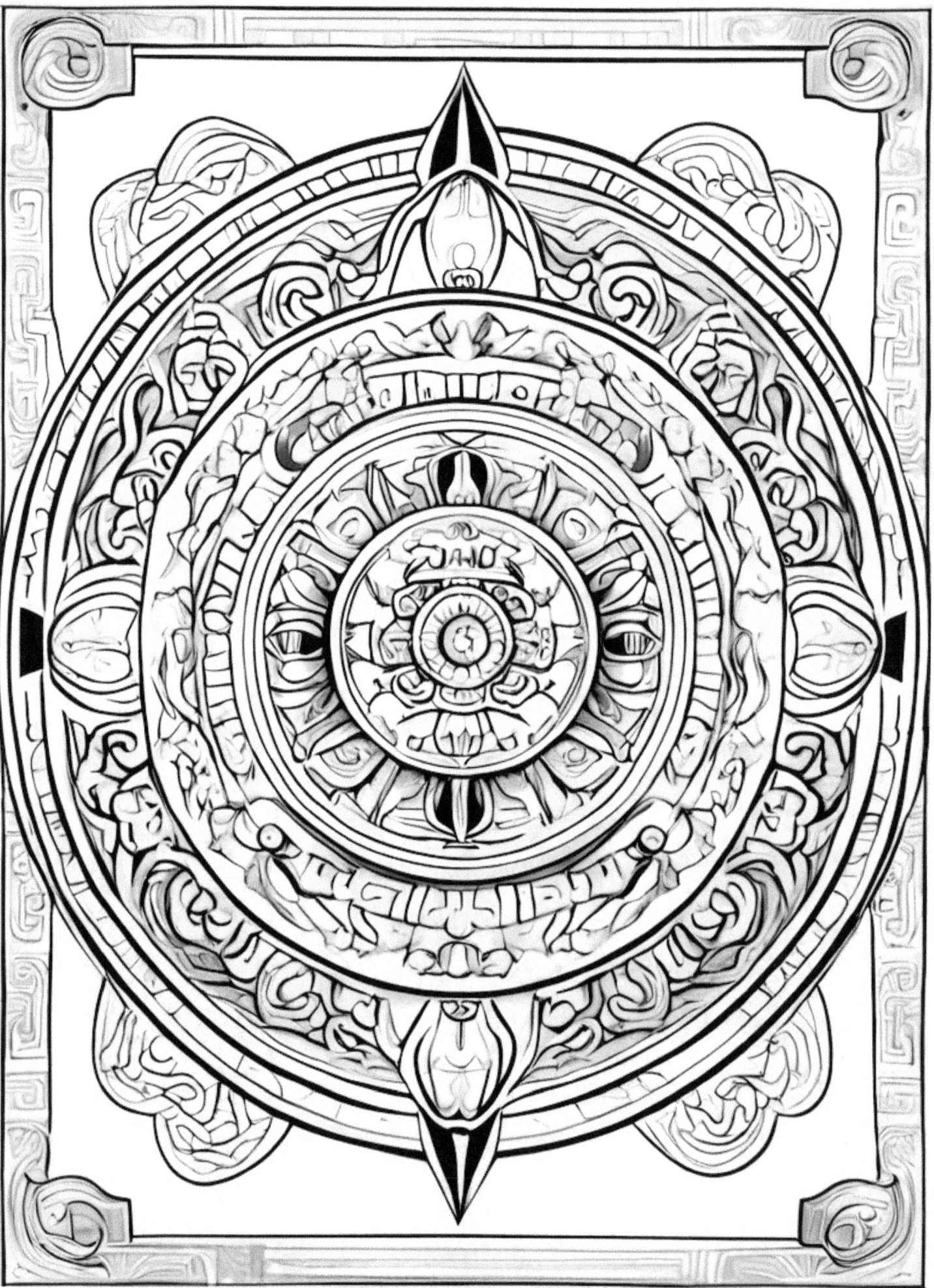

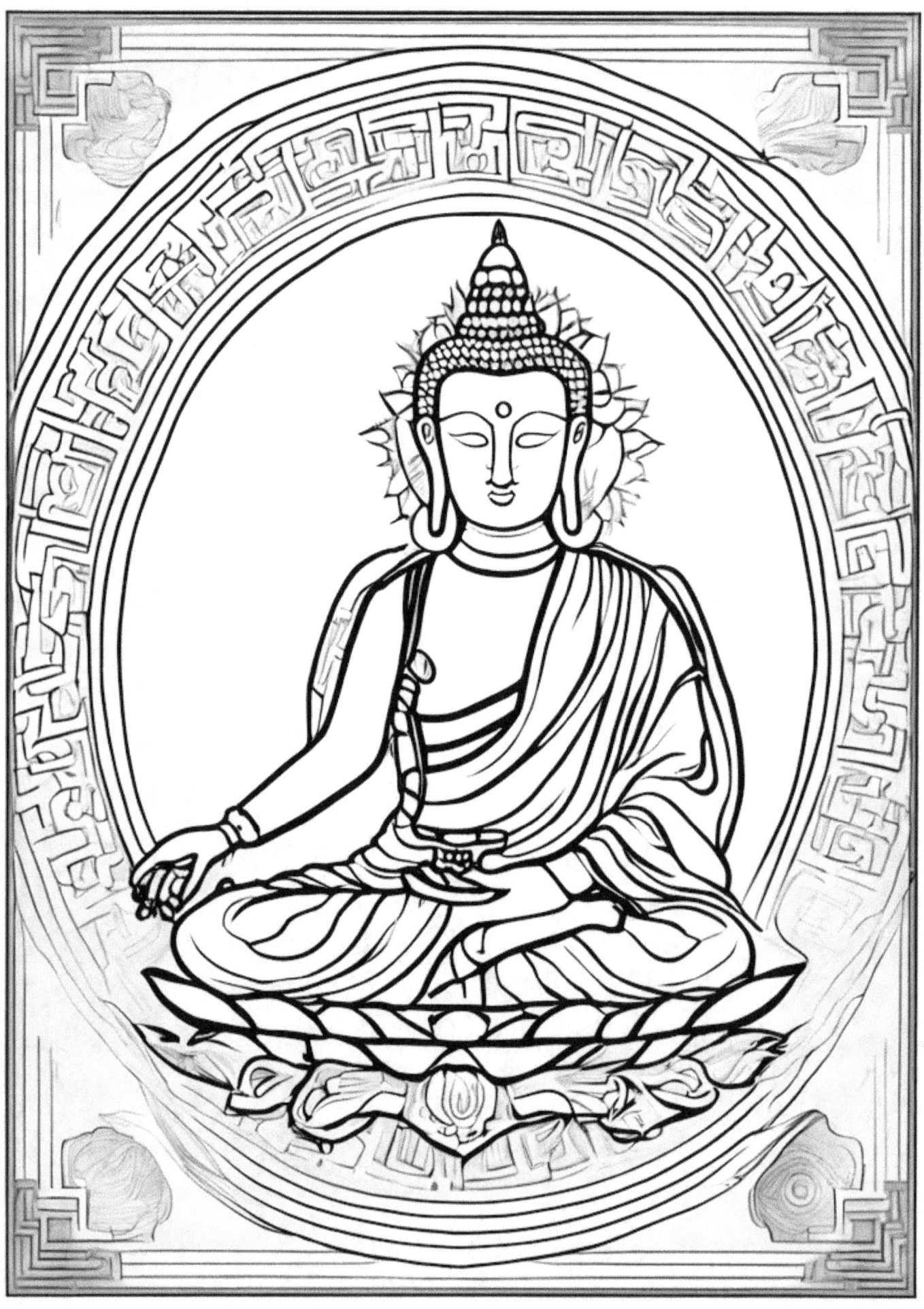

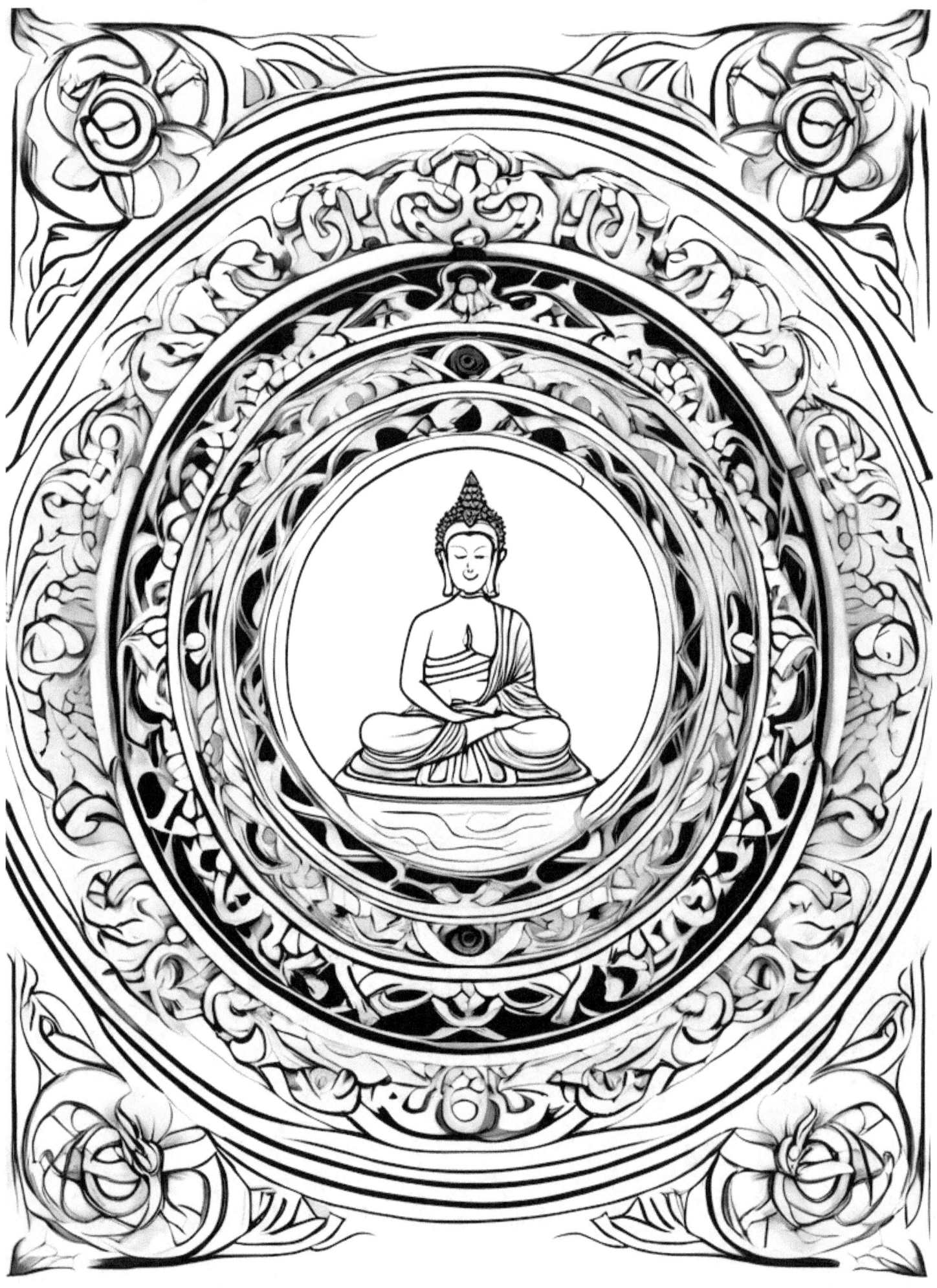

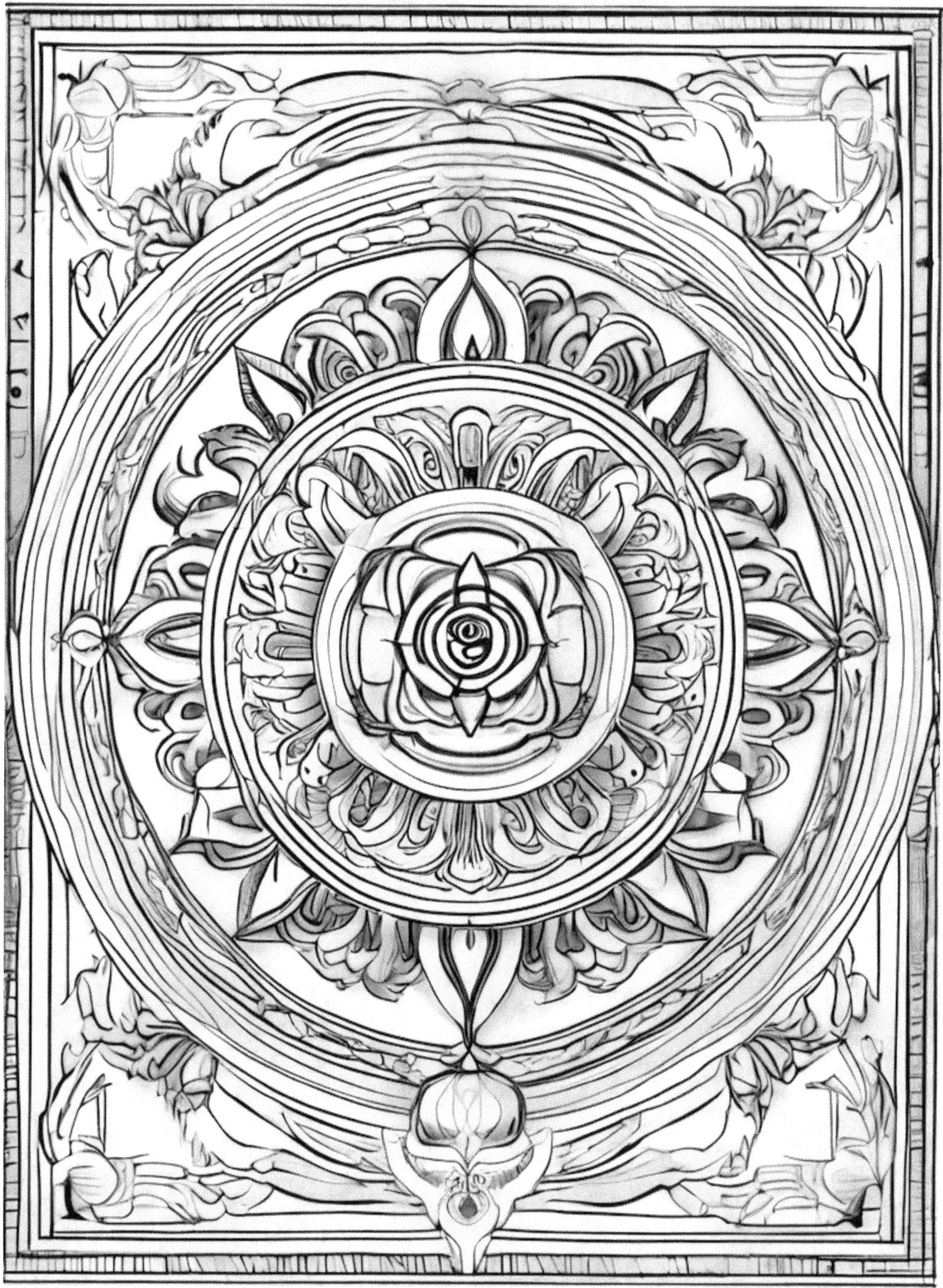

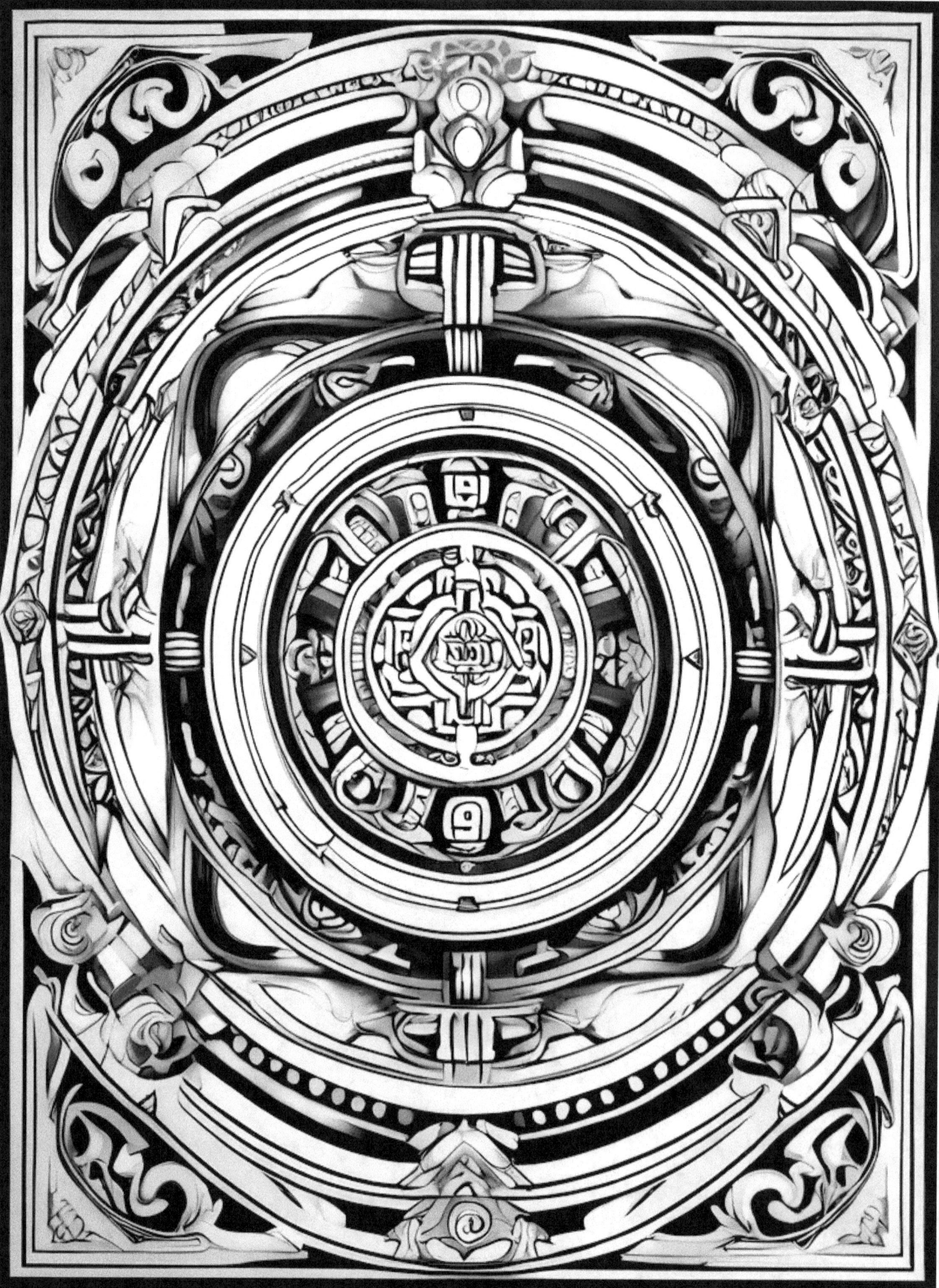

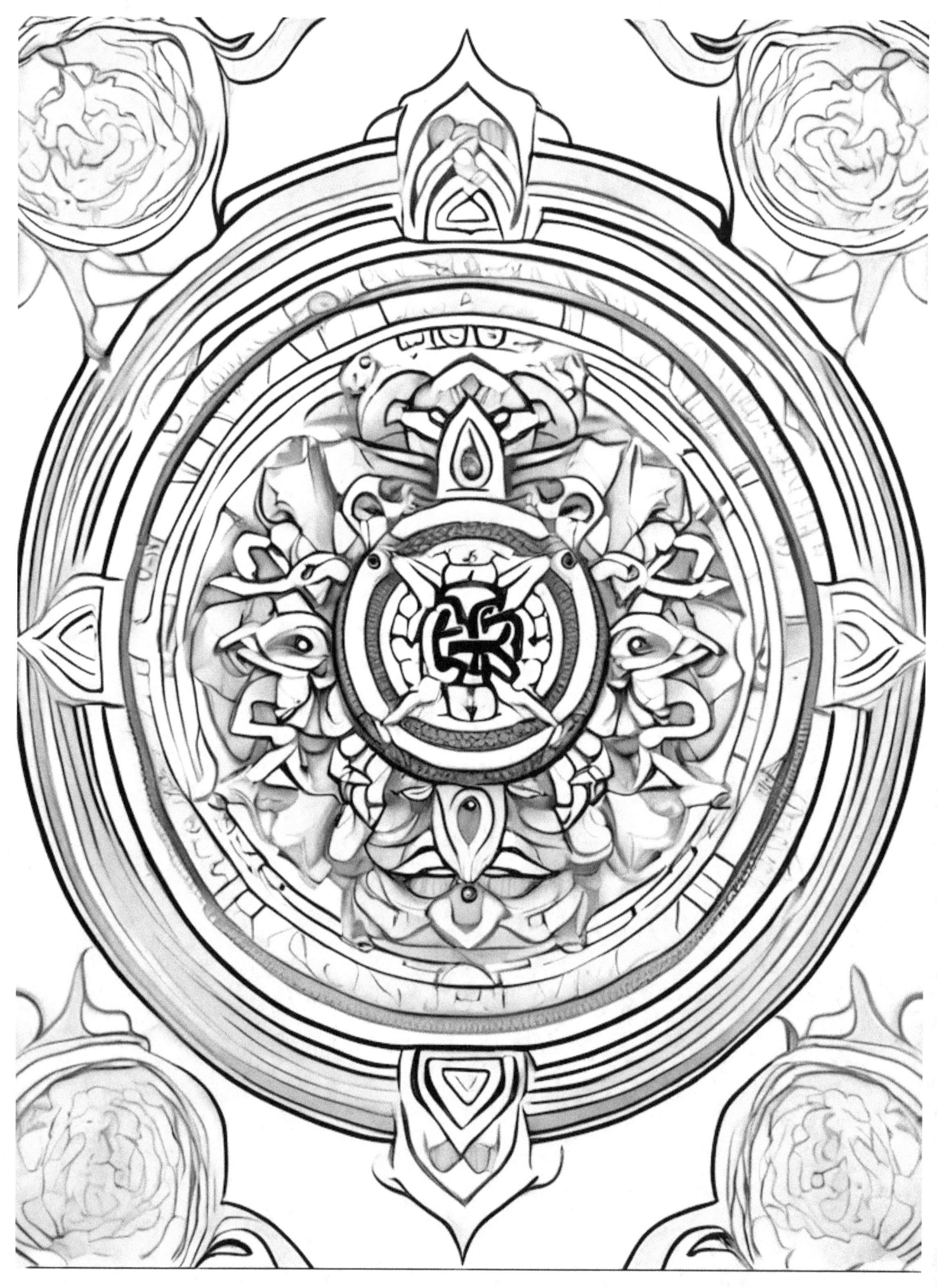

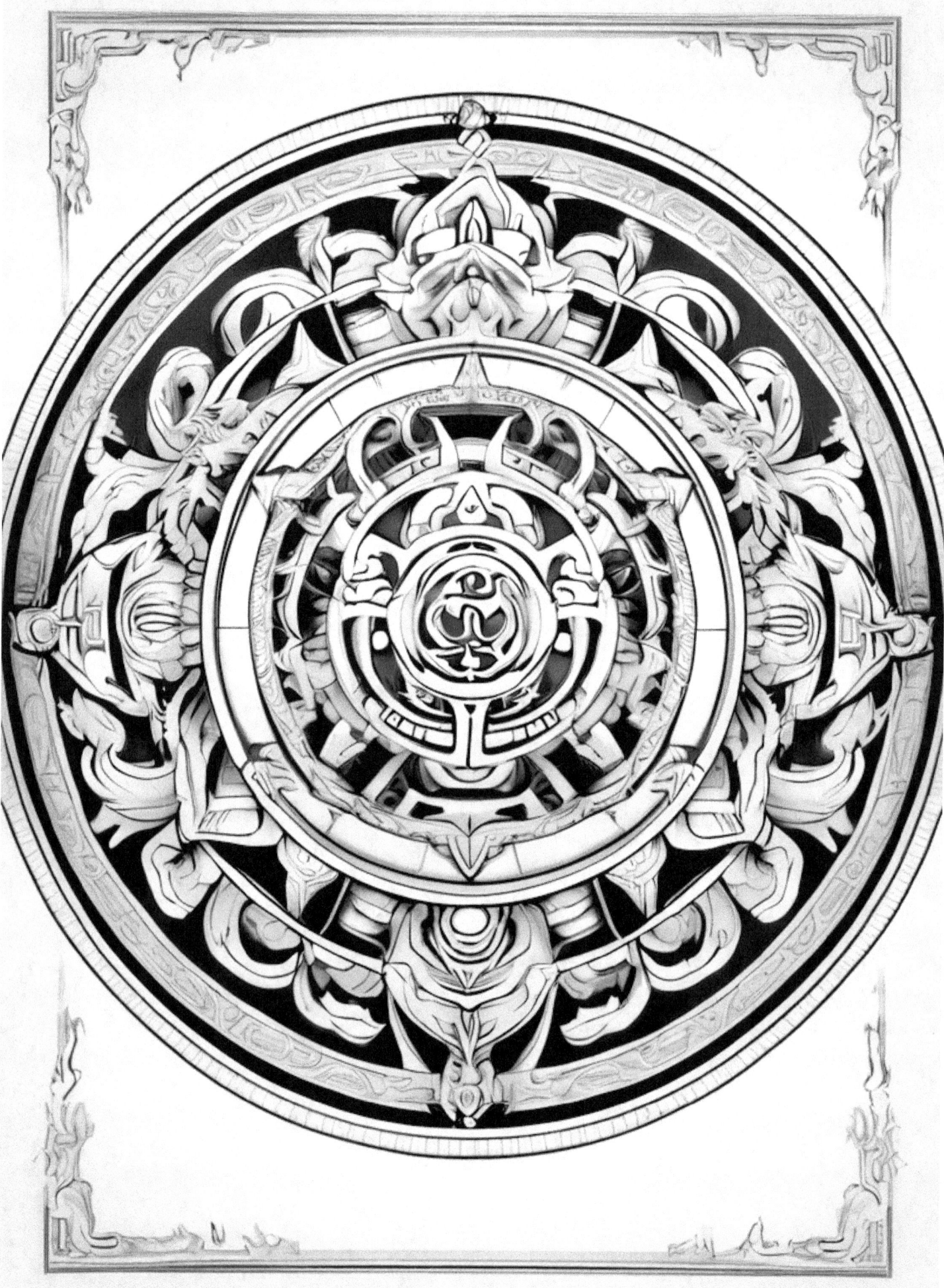

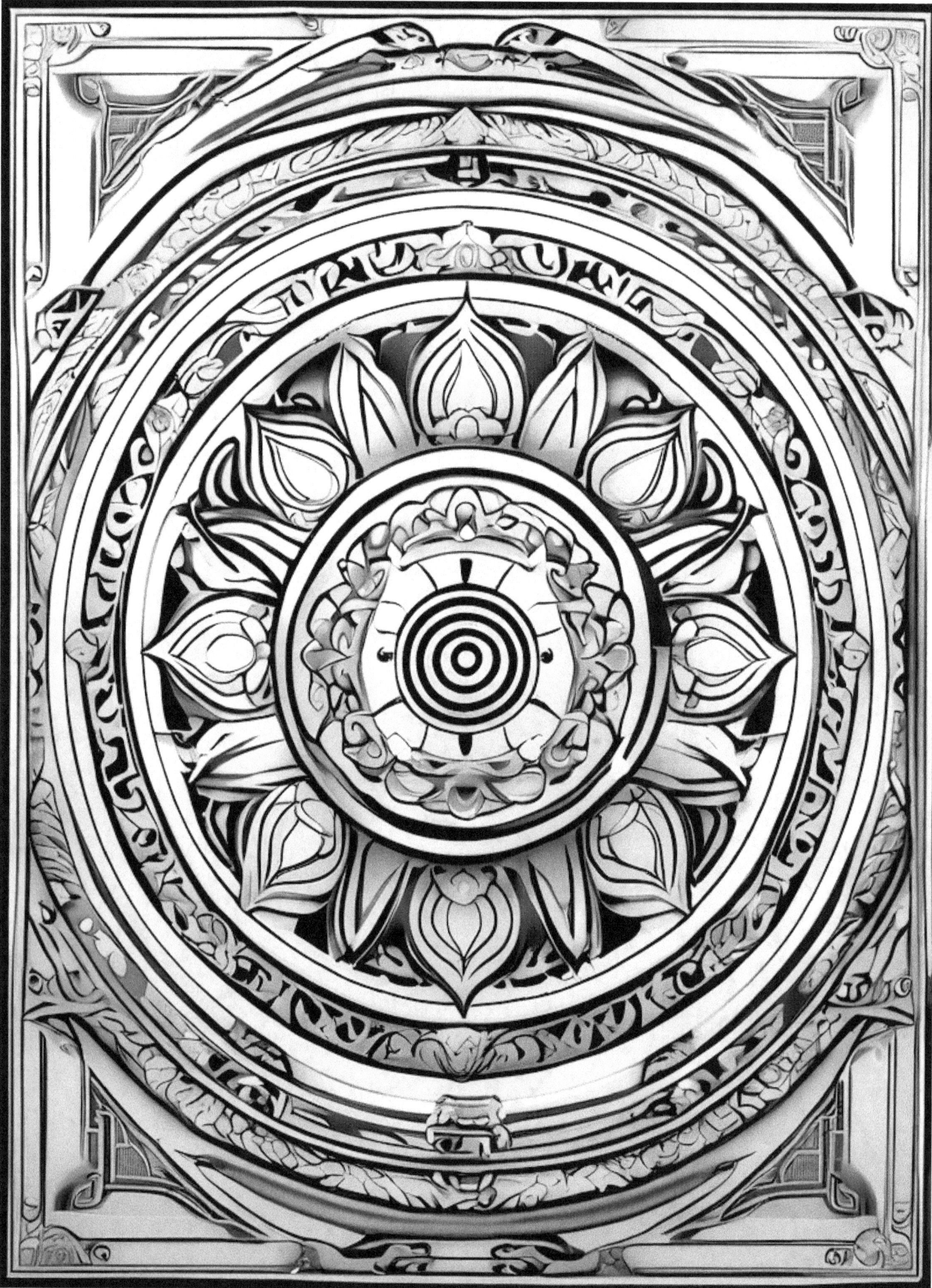

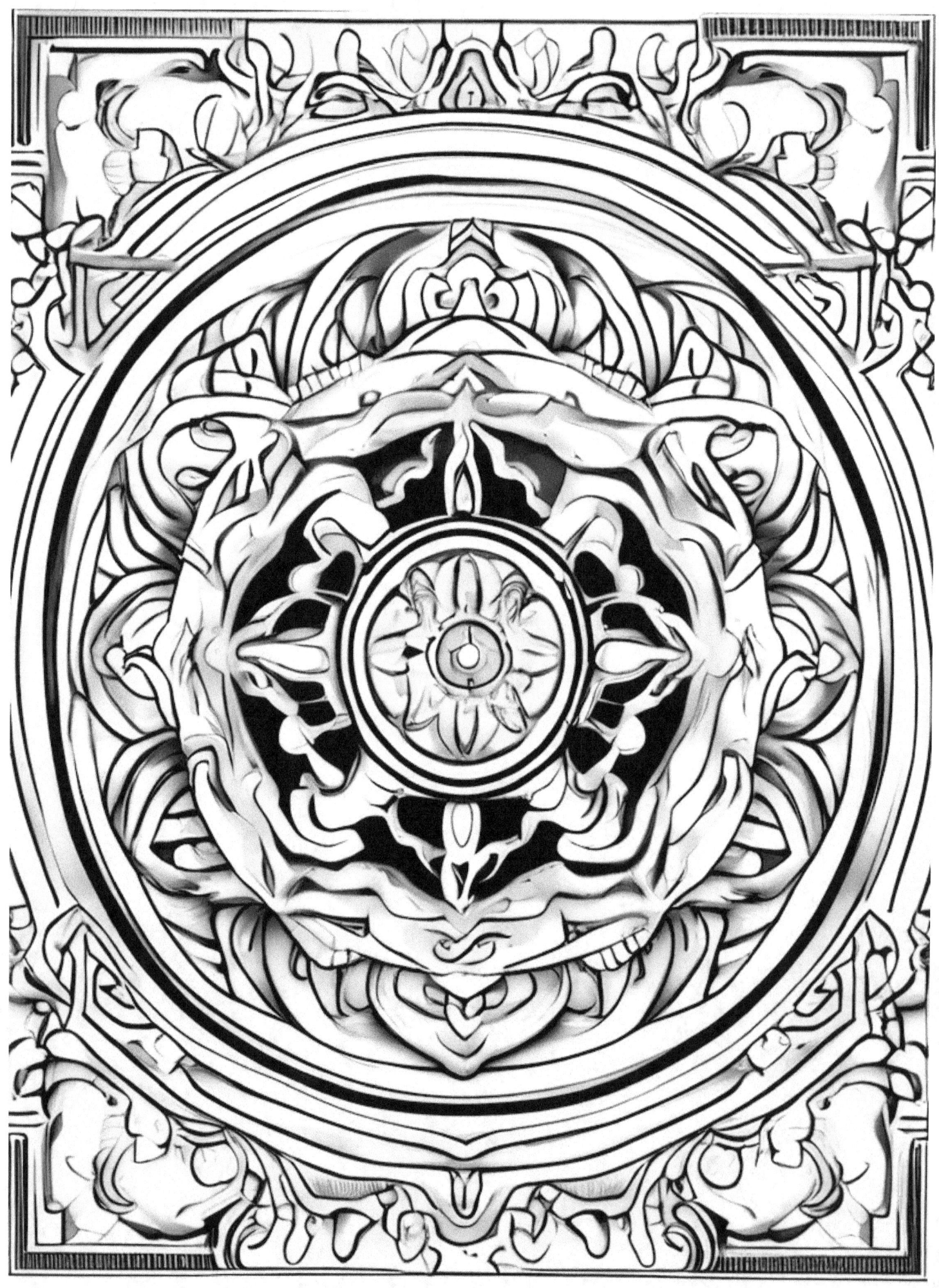

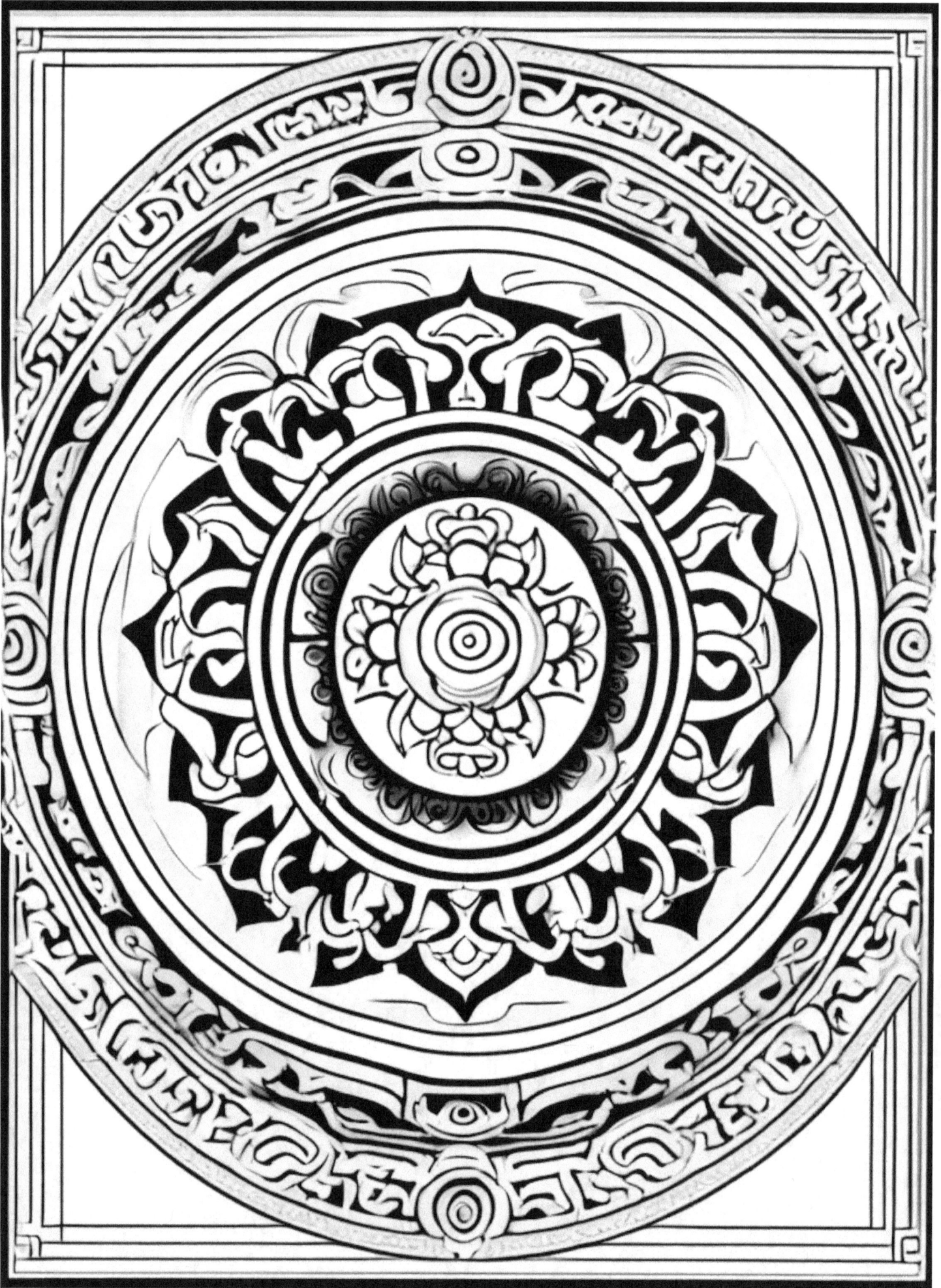

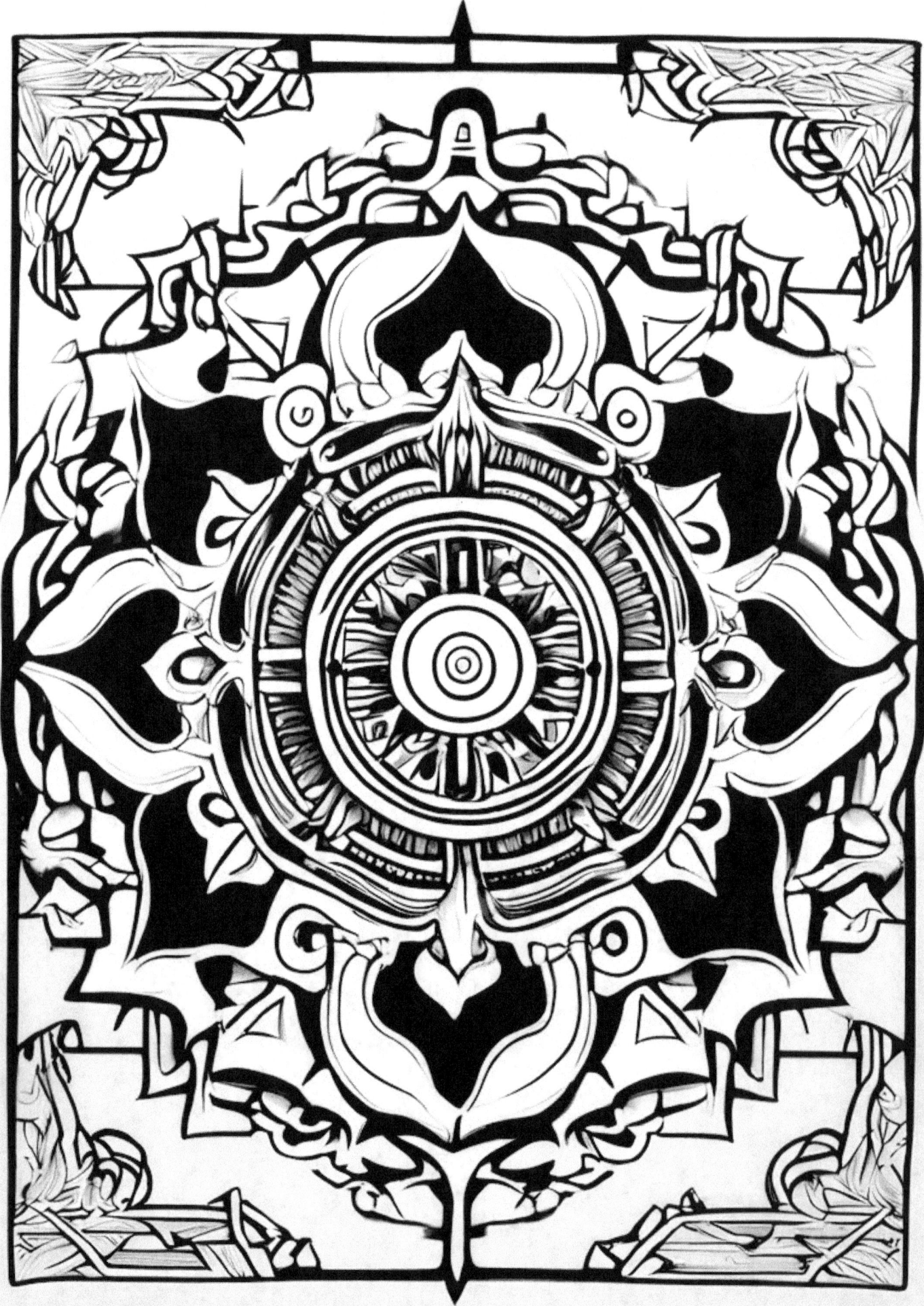

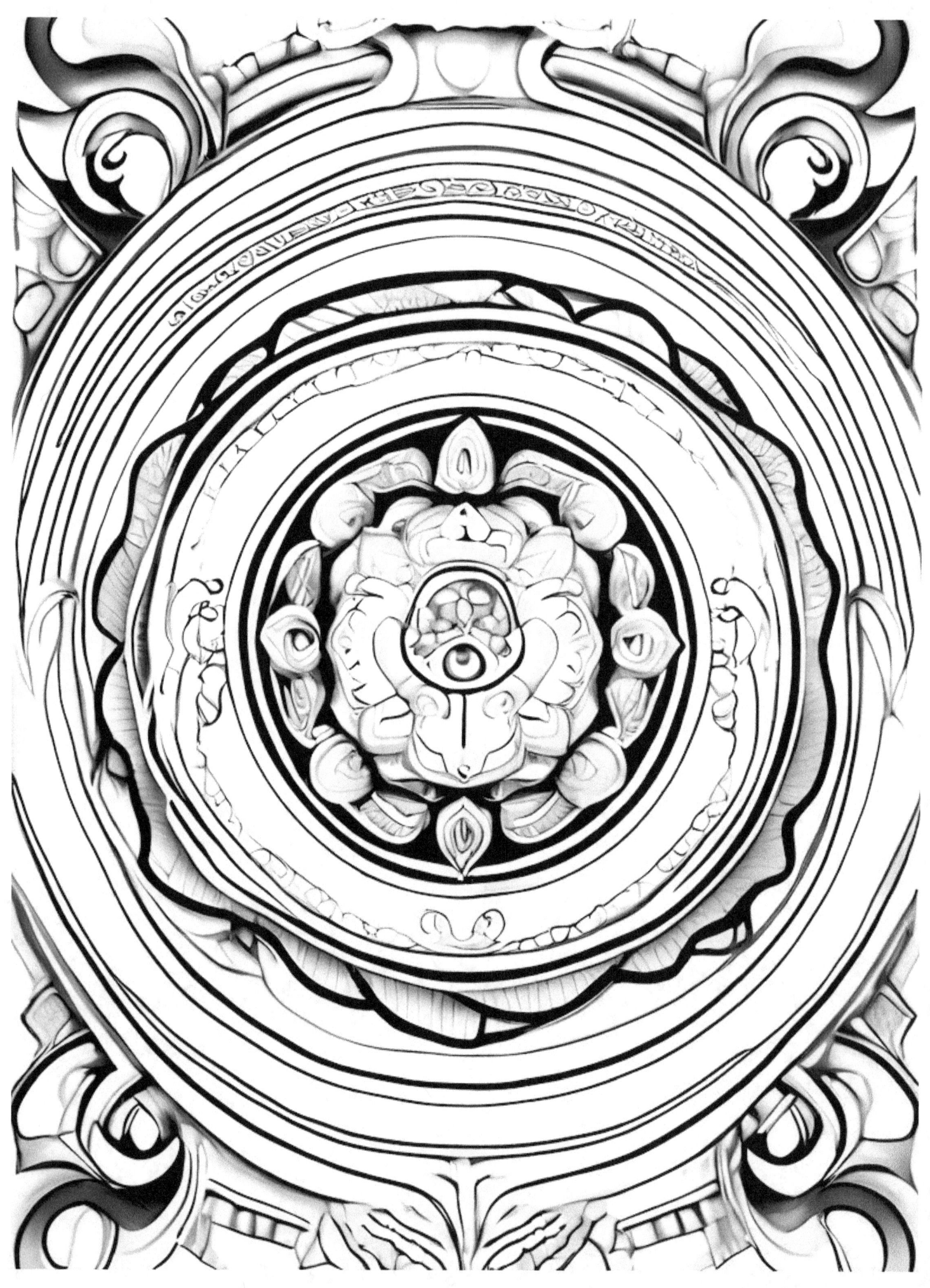

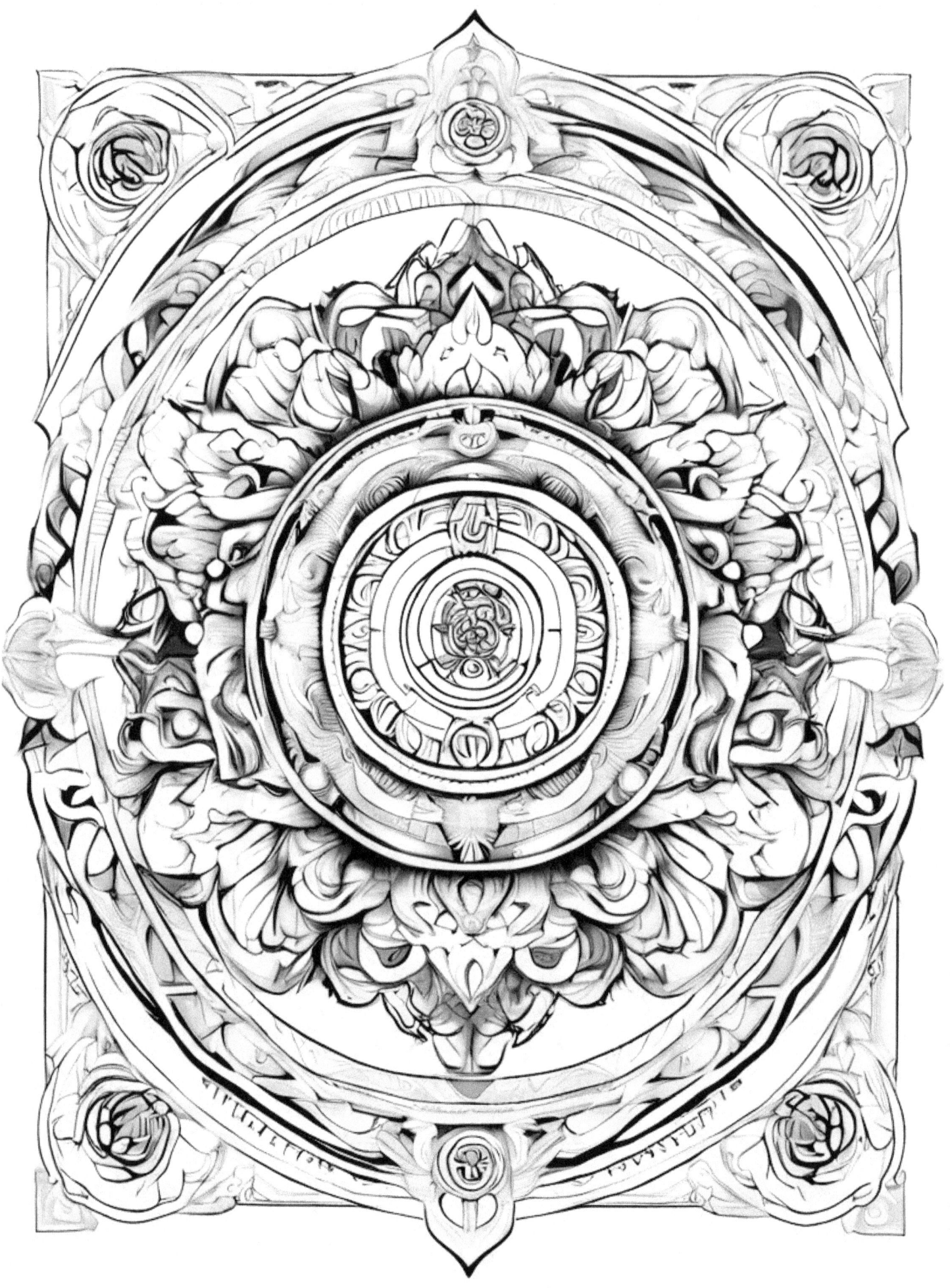

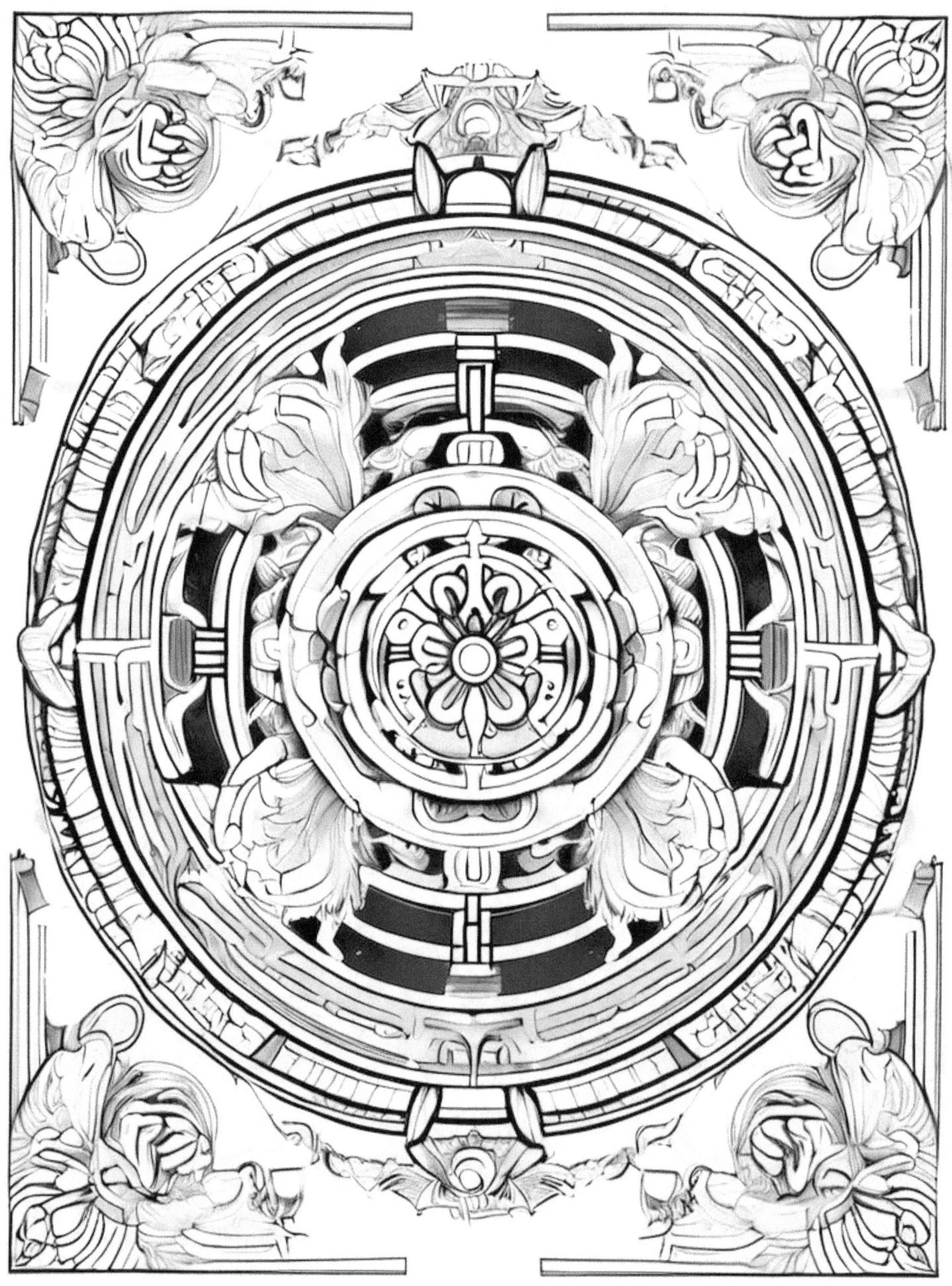

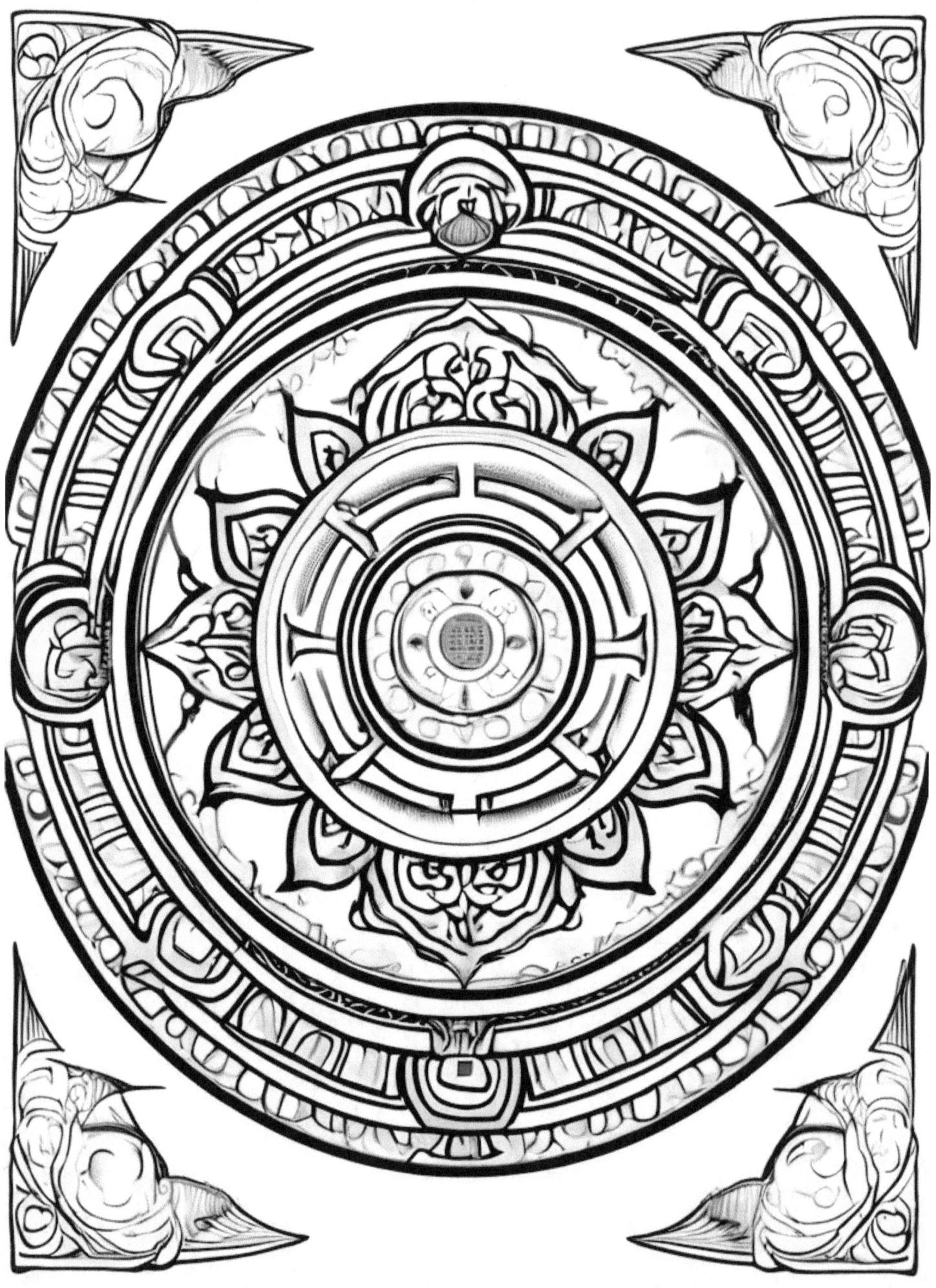

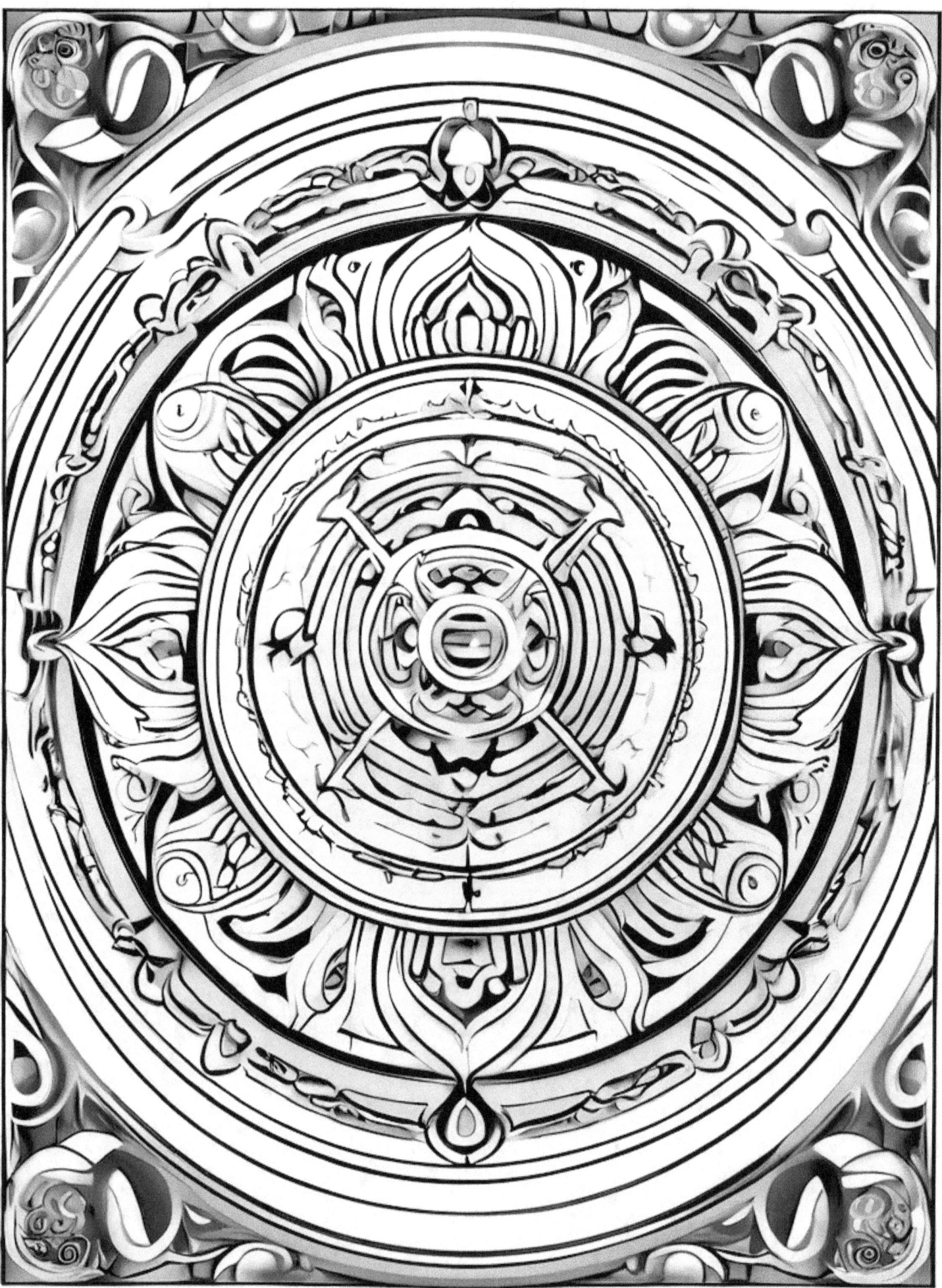

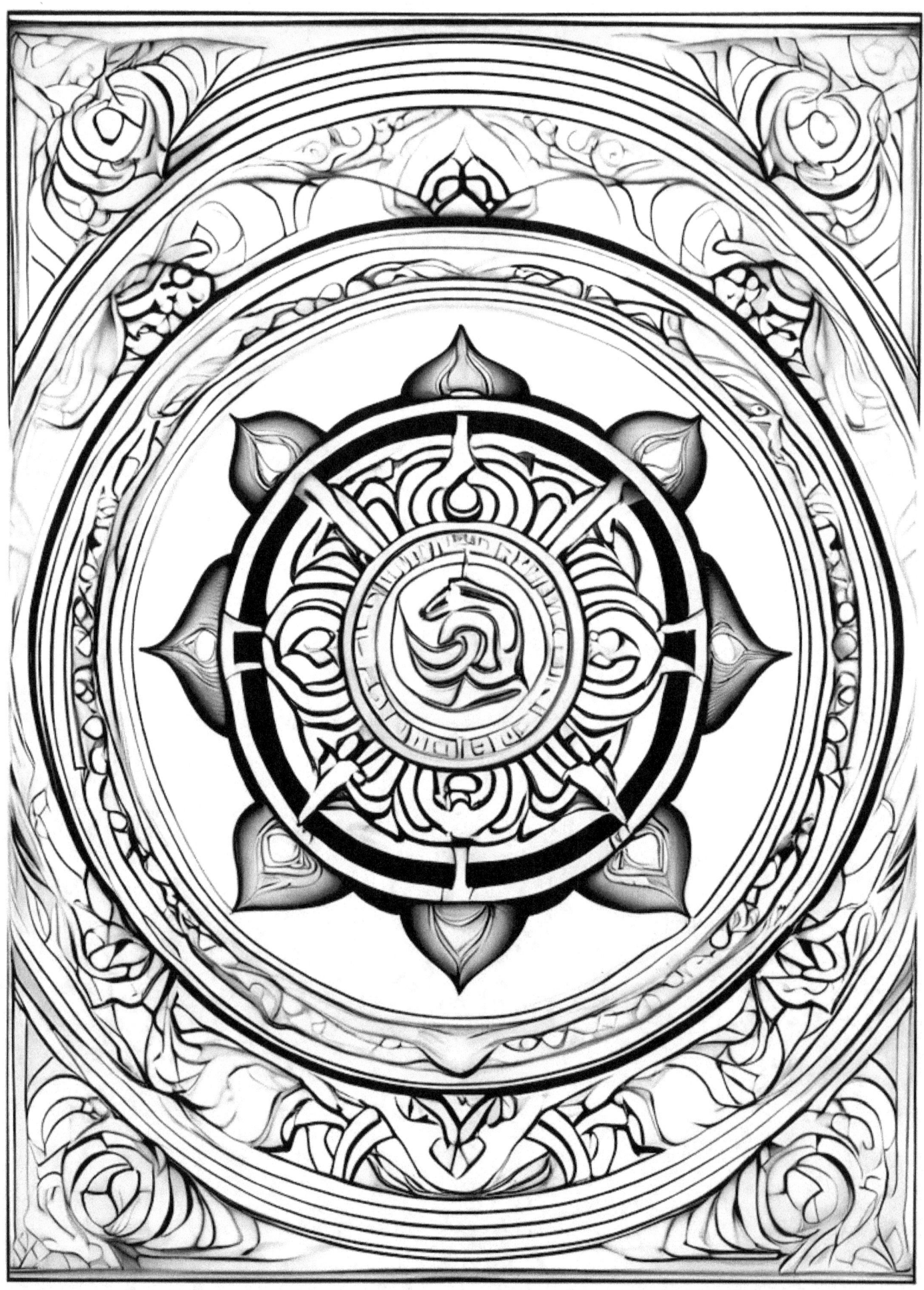

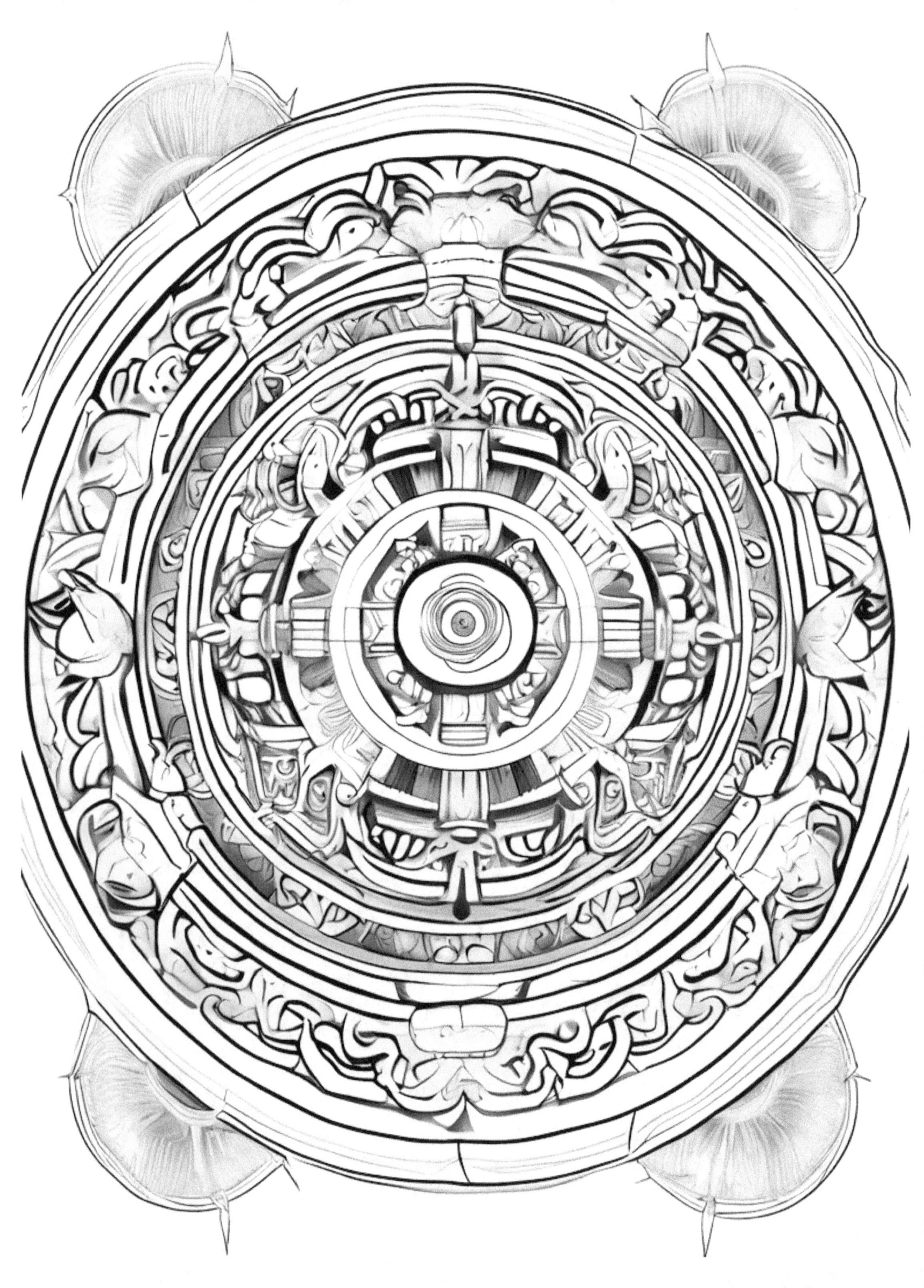

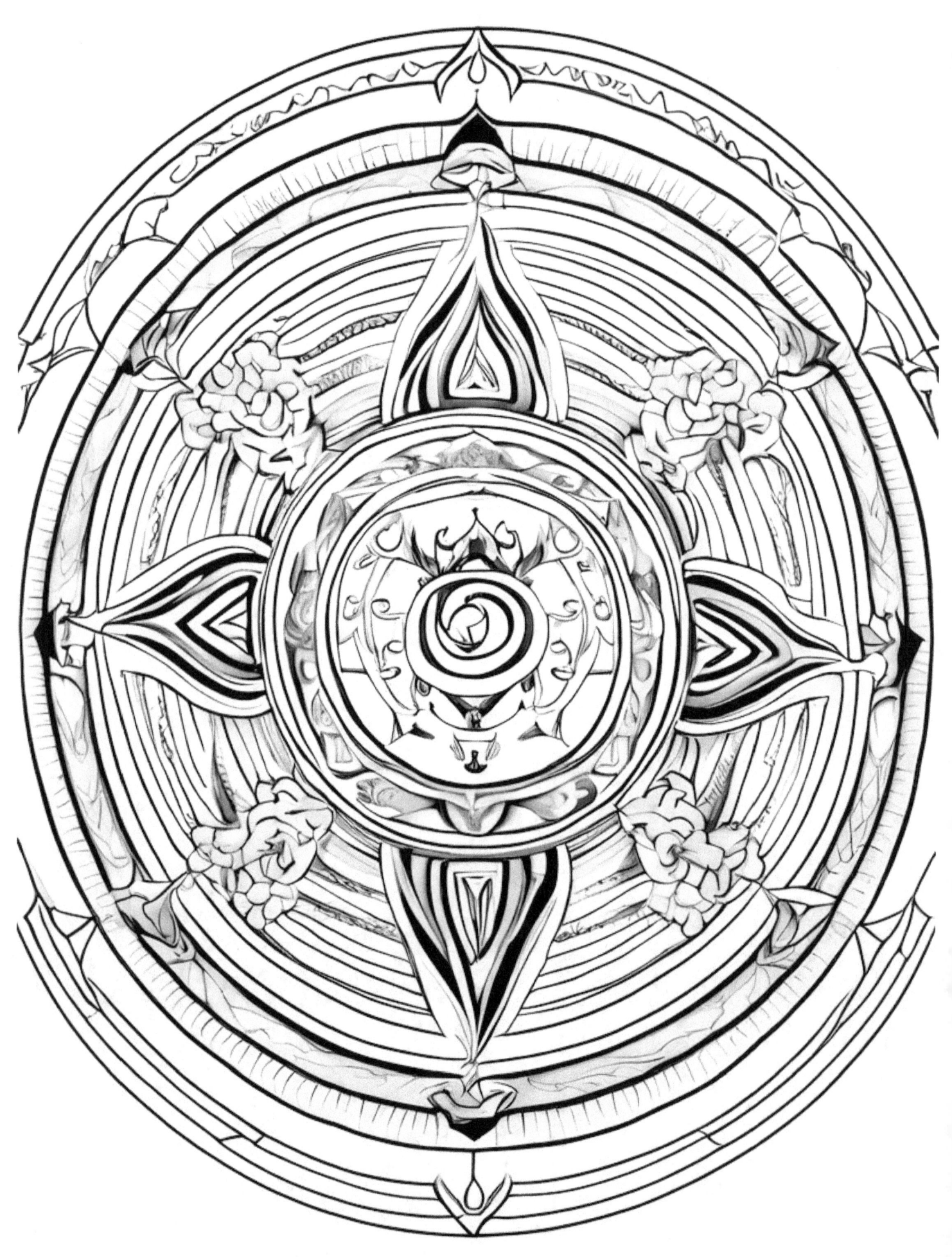

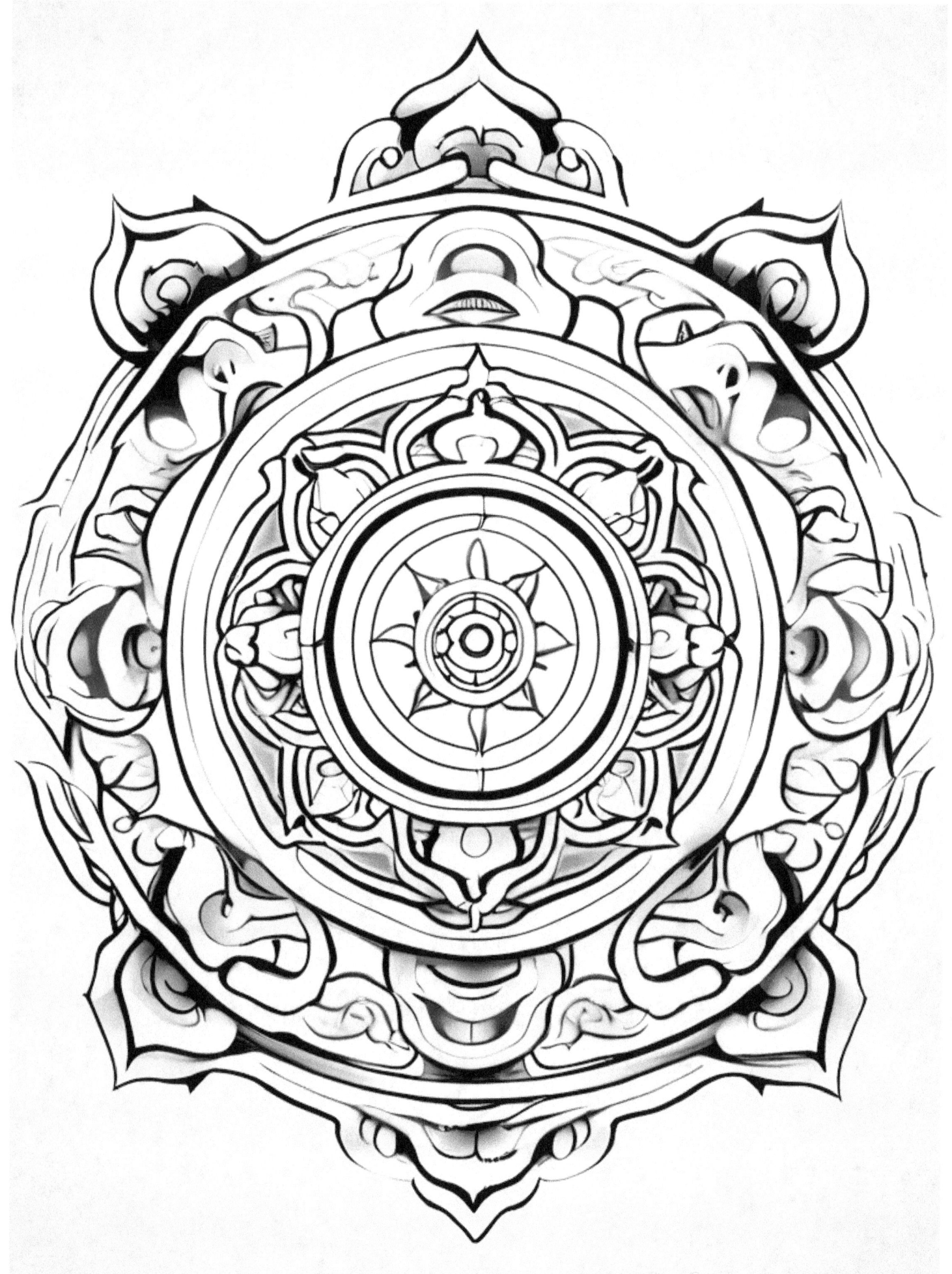

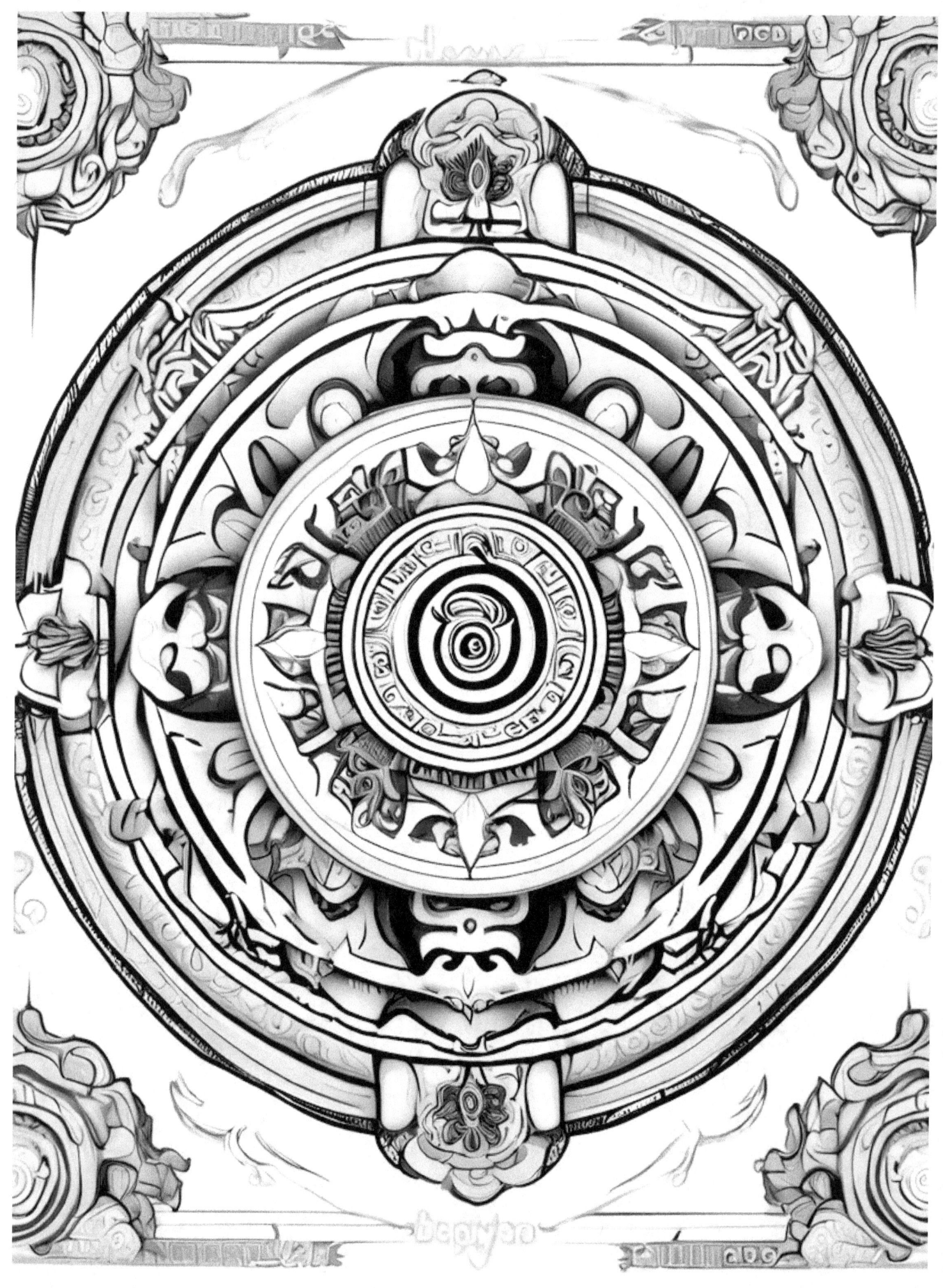

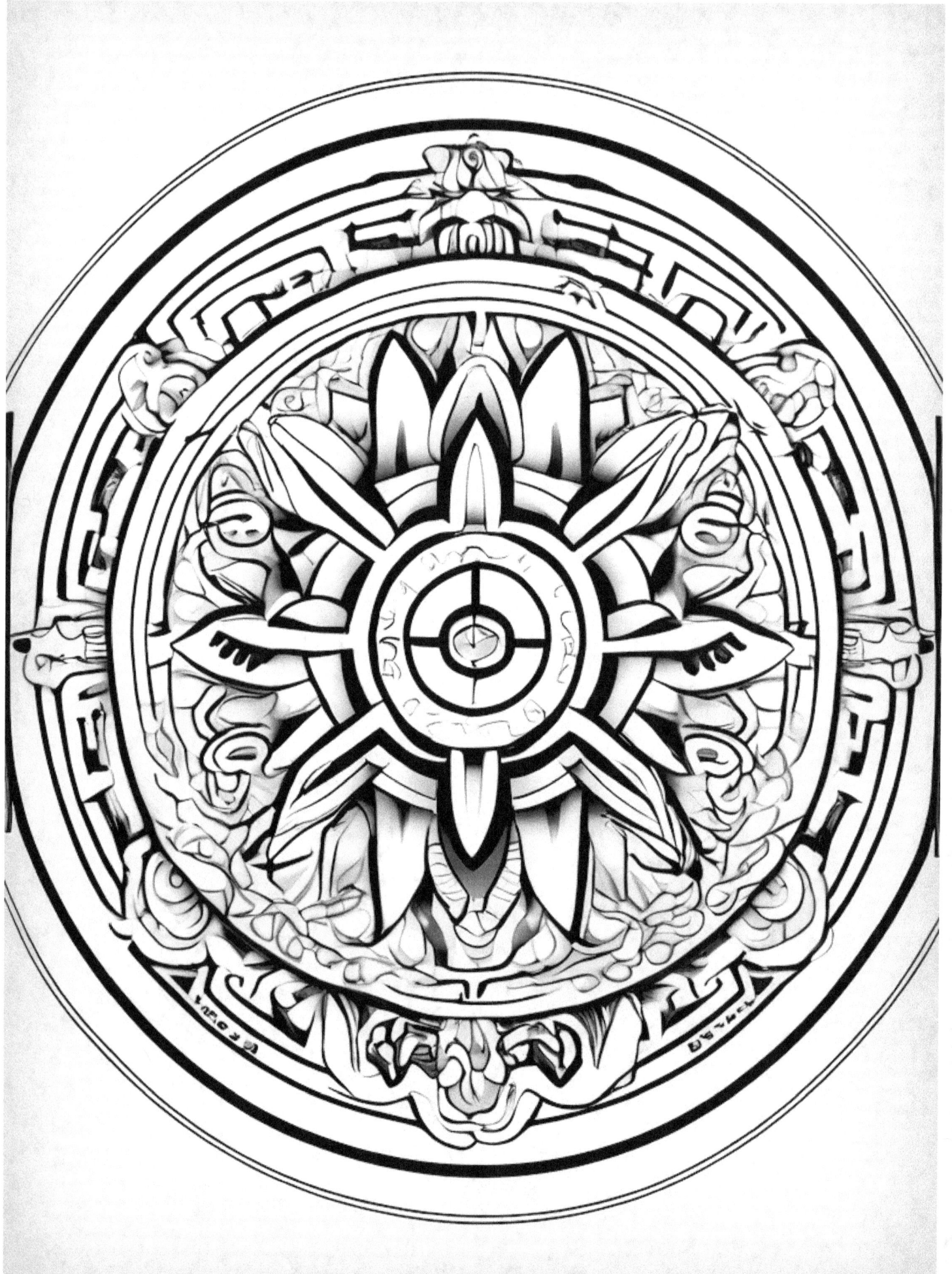

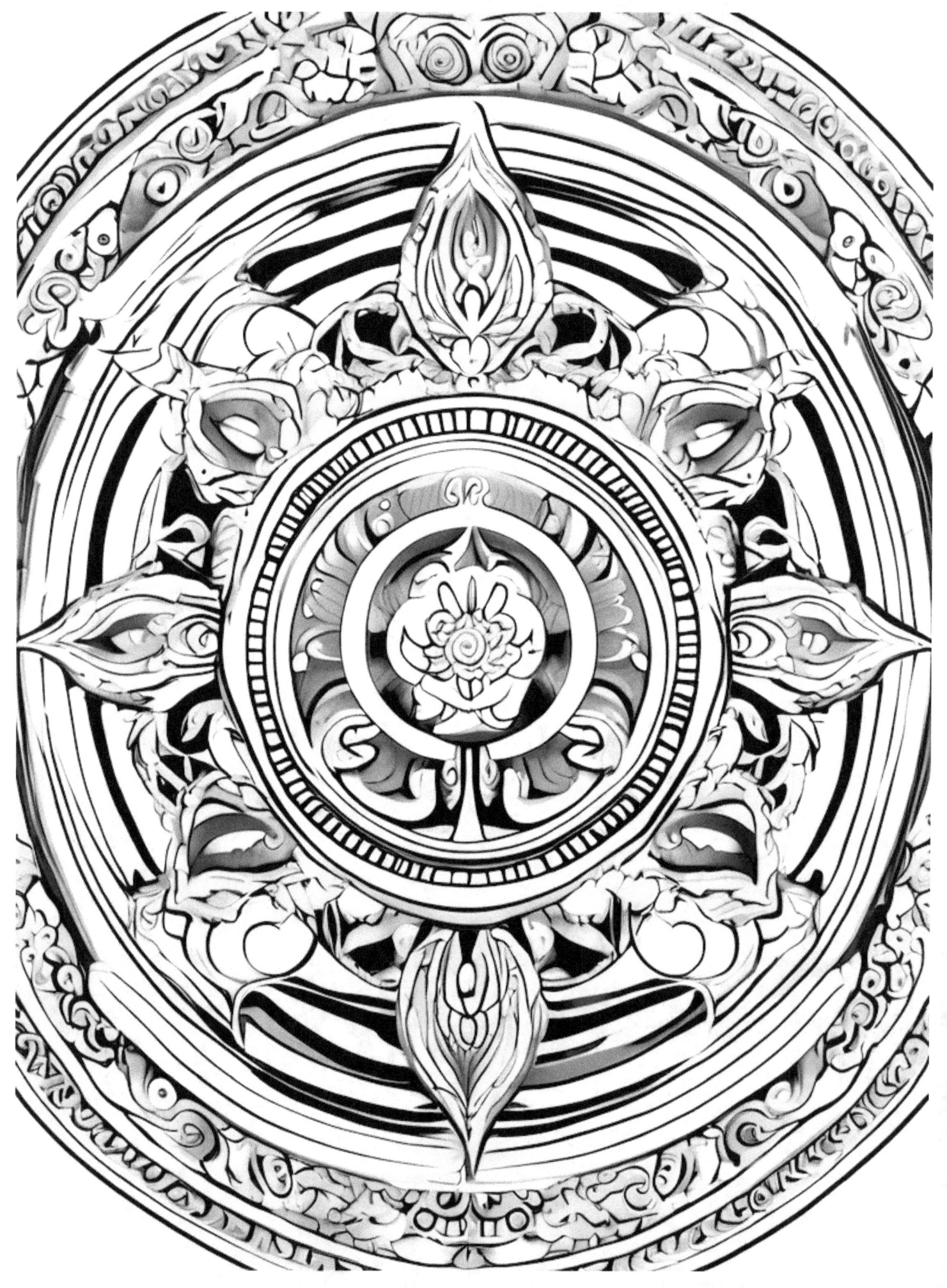

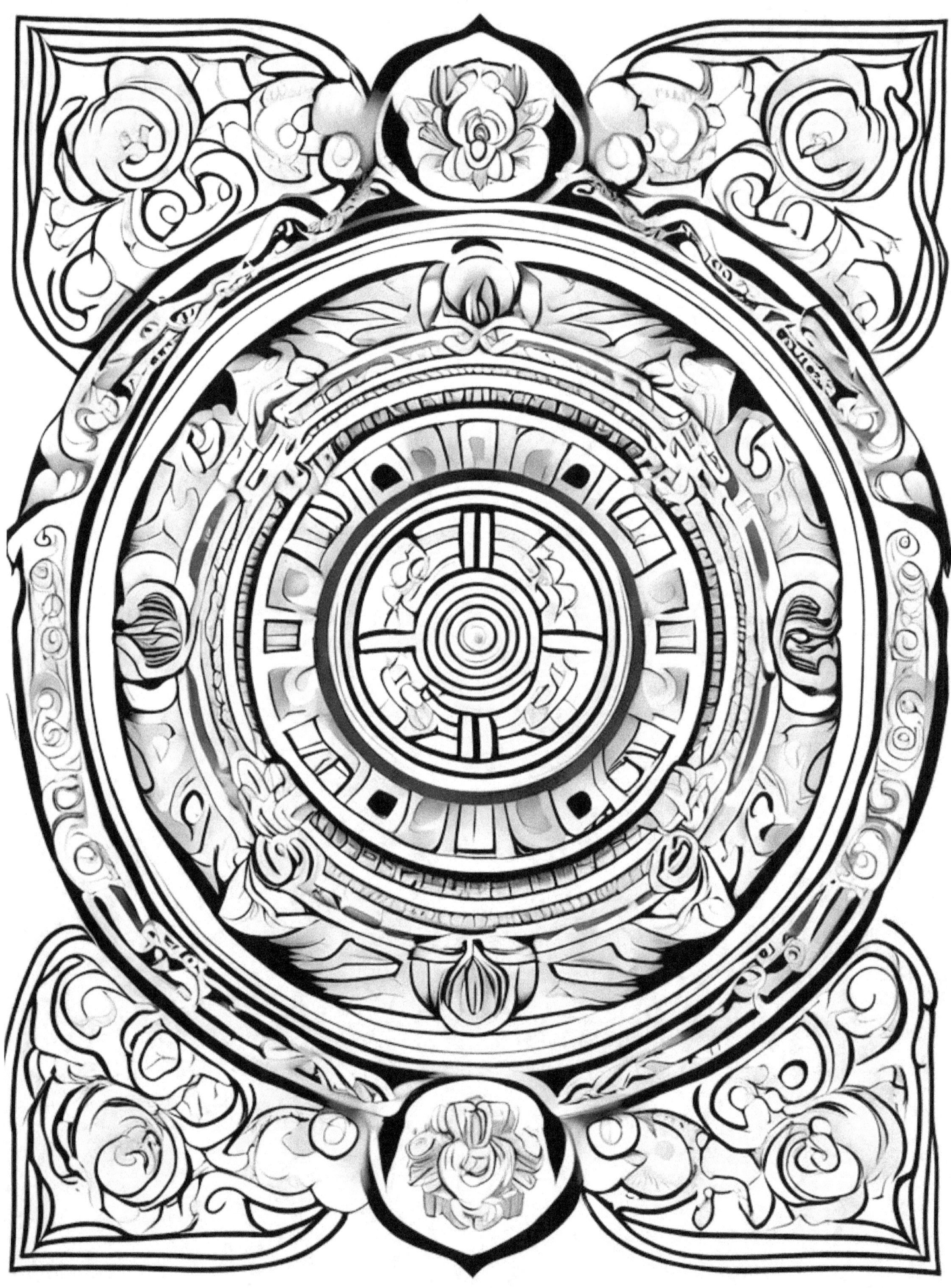

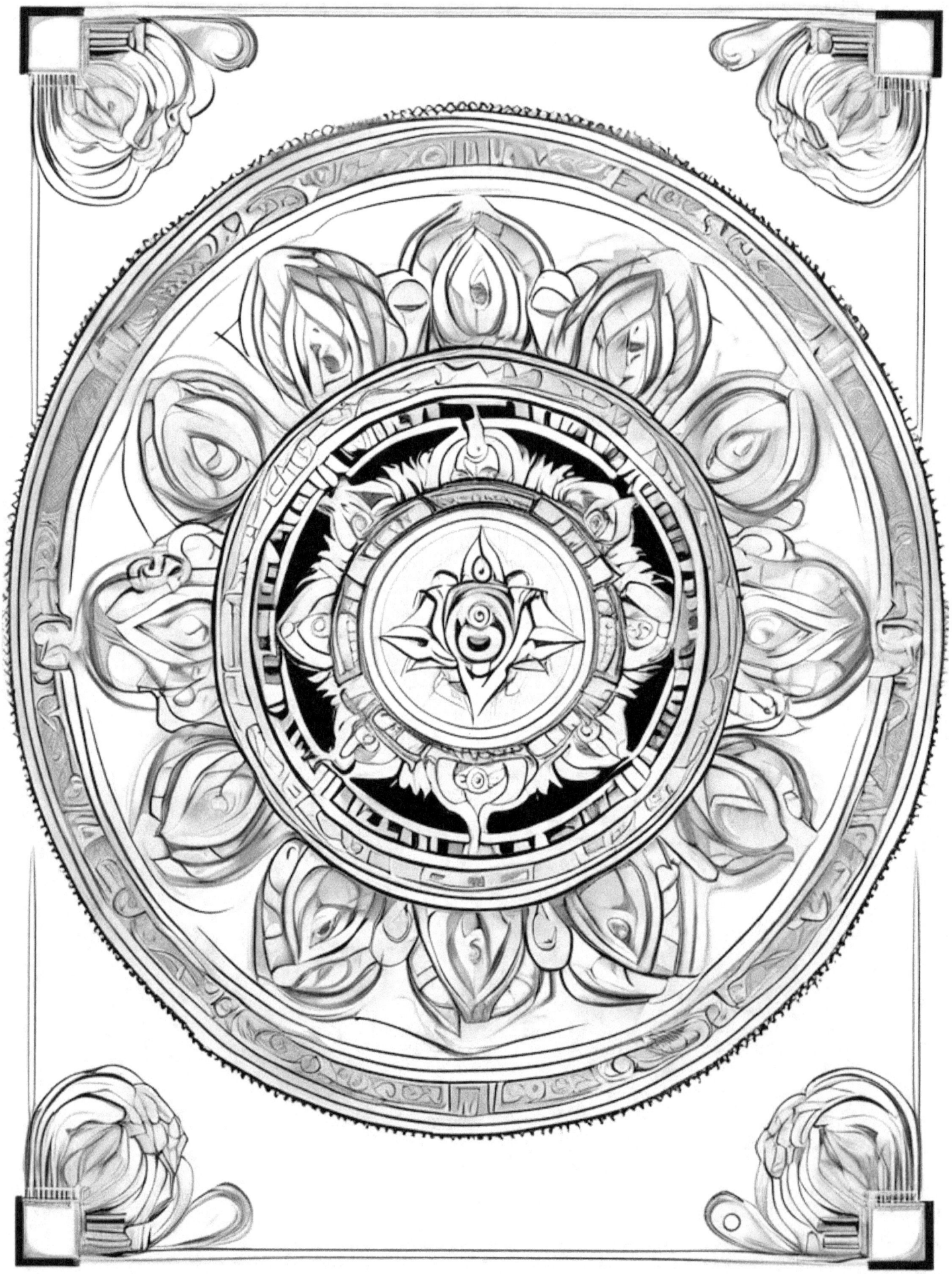

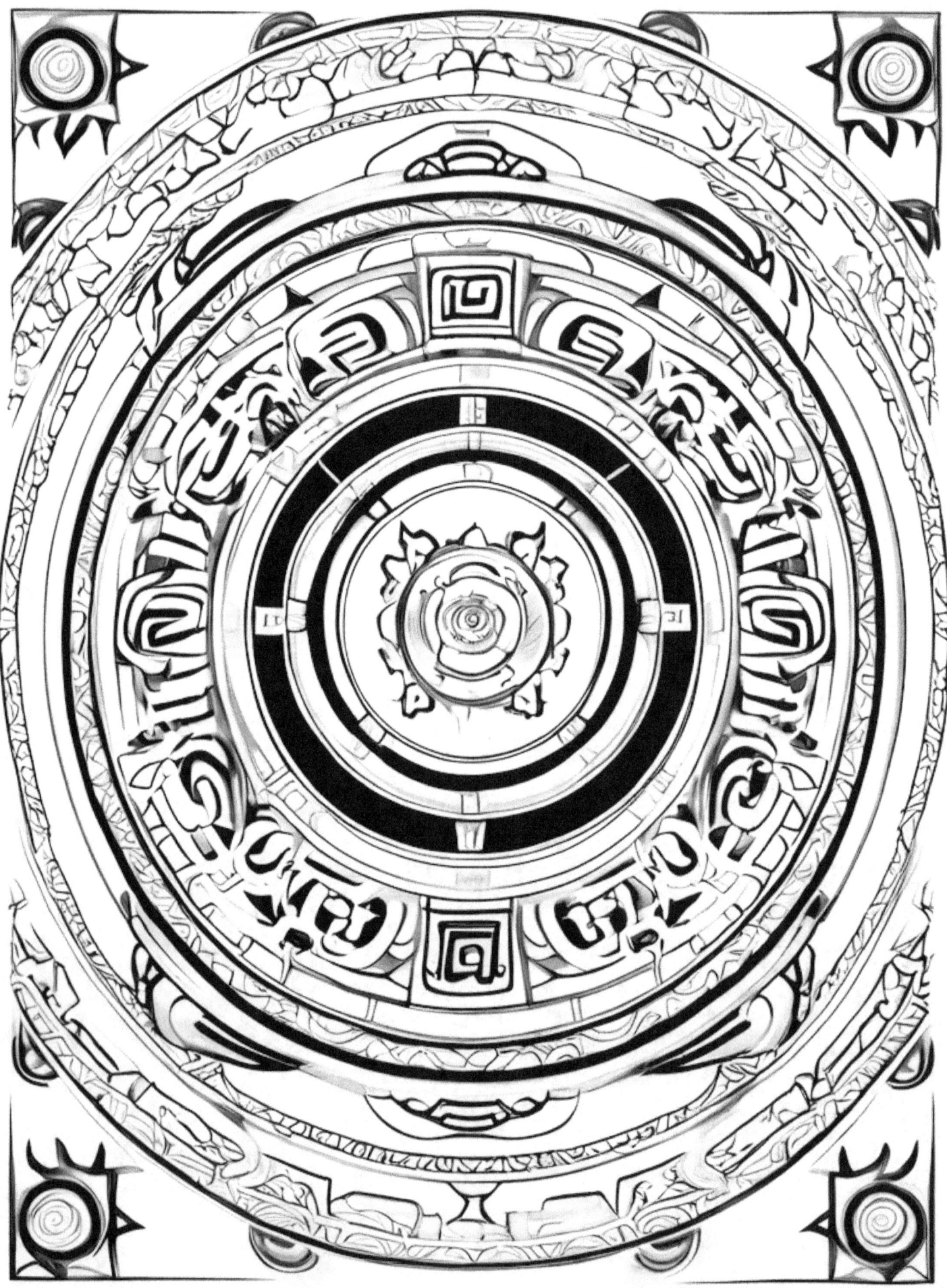

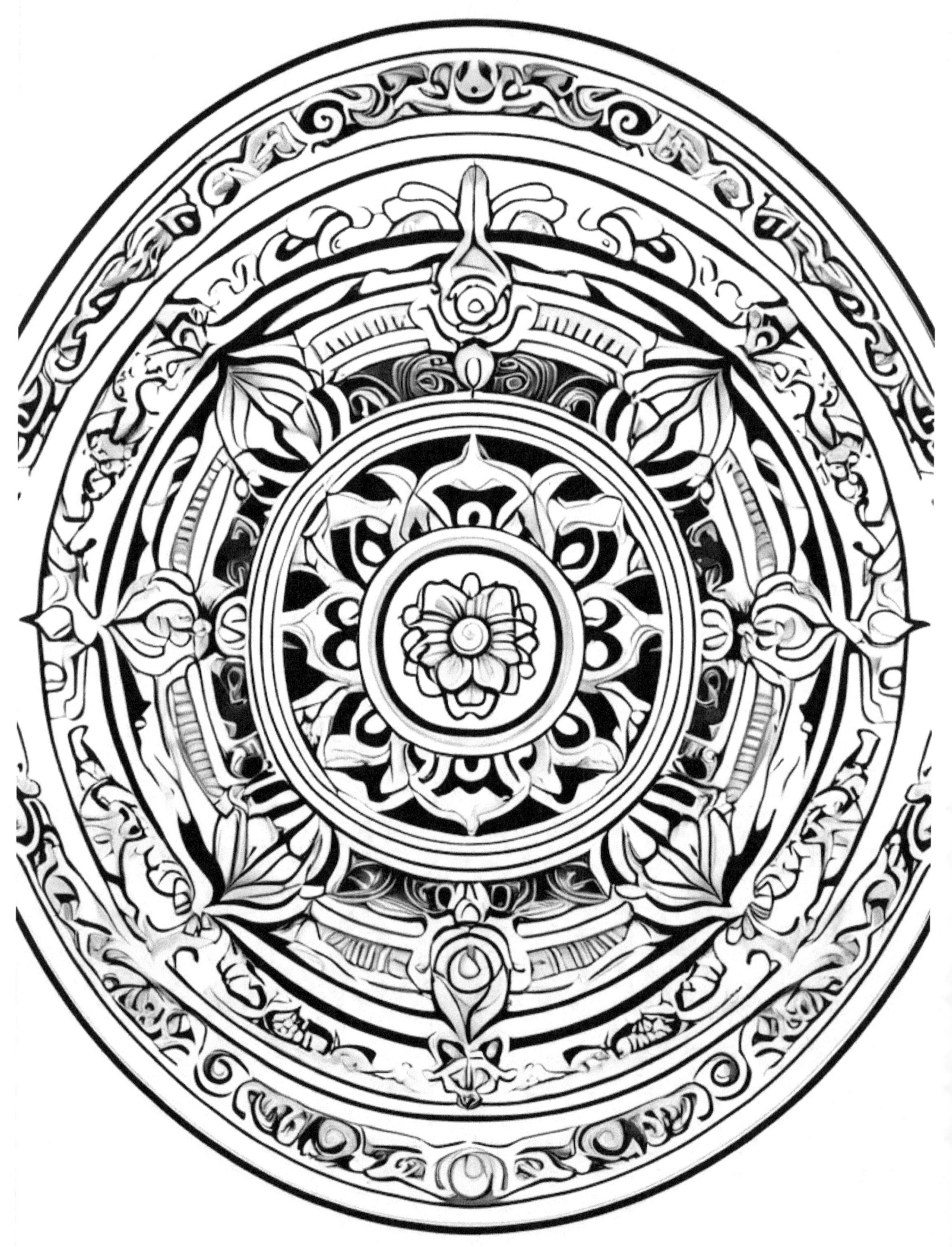

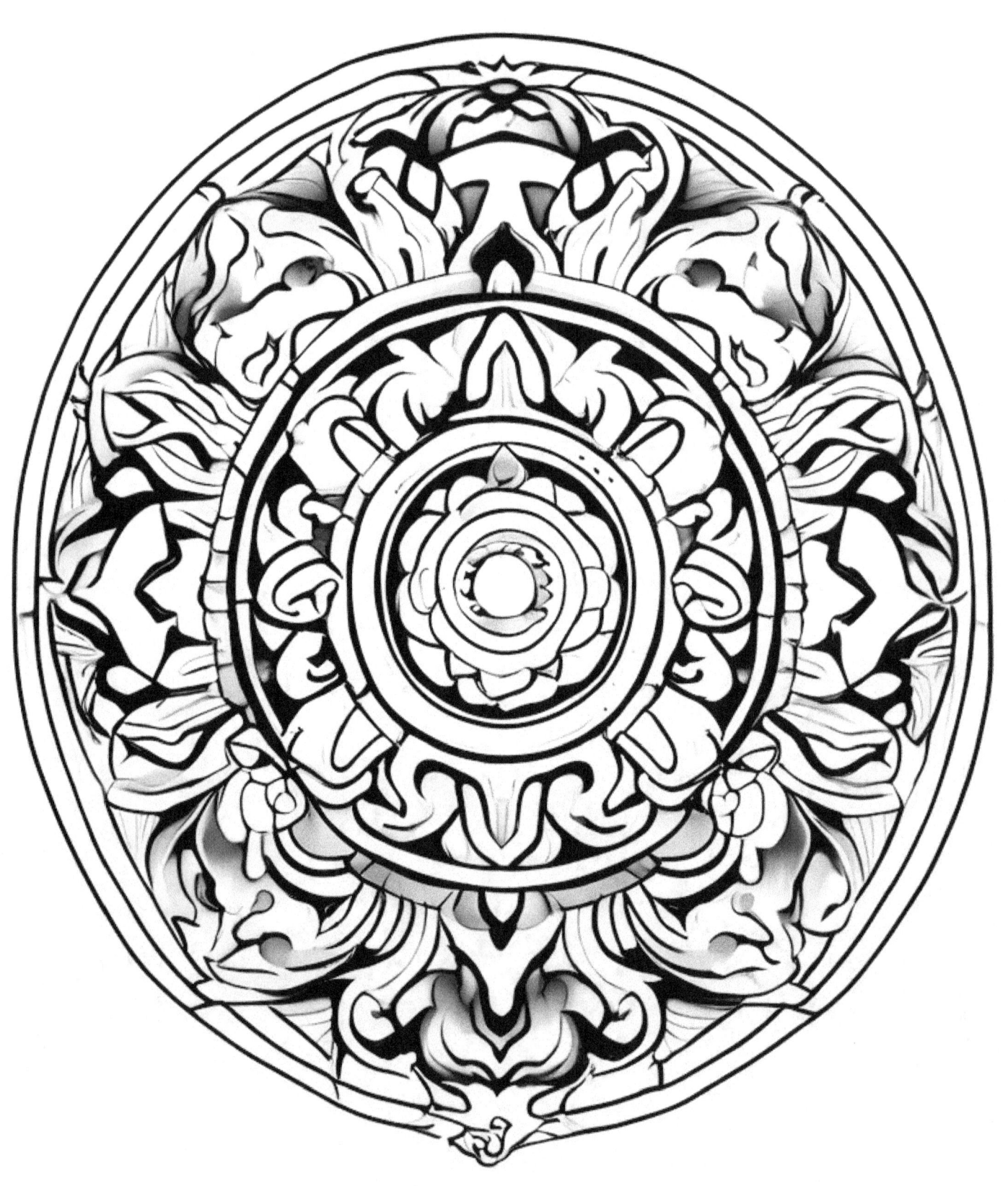

Tibetan mandalas, with their symbolic complexity and intricate patterns, were not mere drawings to fill with color, but portals to tranquility and contemplation.

As you colored each circle, you immersed yourself in a process of active meditation, finding serenity in your brushstrokes.

May your search for harmony continue, painting your life with the vibrant colors of peace.

Namaste.

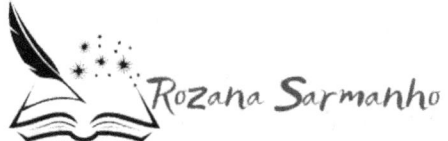

Rozana Sarmanho